GOD IS MY BUSINESS PLAN

A GUIDEBOOK FOR ENTREPRENEURS

KEIRA POULSEN

GOD IS MY BUSINESS PLAN
A GUIDEBOOK FOR ENTREPRENEURS
Copyright © 2022 by Keira Poulsen

To request permissions, contact the publisher at
contact@freedomhousepublishingco.com or contact@keirapoulsen.com.
Hardback ISBN: 978-1-952566-80-6
Paperback ISBN: 978-1-952566-81-3
Ebook ISBN: 978-1-952566-82-0

Printed in the USA.
Freedom House Publishing Co
Middleton, ID 83644
www.freedomhousepublishingco.com

BONUS MAGIC

This guidebook is **more** than just a book.

It is an interactive experience.

I have created meditations, healing codex practices, and videos to support your path through this book and your entrepreneurial journey.

*Click the QR code below
to get immediate access to this
BONUS MAGIC!*

*xo
Keira*

PRAISE FOR KEIRA POULSEN

"Keira Poulsen's gift is her ability to get people who are facing creative blocks to get unstuck. Whether you're trying to write a book, choreograph a dance, design a logo, parent a child, start a business... if it requires creativity, and you're feeling stuck, Keira can help. She helped channel my book and I wrote it in 5 days compared to the one year it took me to write my first book. She helped channel my cover when I had a totally different design in mind. She gets you out of your head and into your heart so you can move from overthinking and get into momentum. If the typical business plans, PowerPoint presentations, and online courses aren't working for you, Keira's approach might just be exactly what you need to unlock your creativity and impact the world."

-**Evan Carmichael, Author of** *Momentum,*
Built to Serve, **and** *Your One Word*
www.evancarmichael.com

"I've known Keira for 4 years. When I first met her, she had nothing but dreams. But as she always does, she was ALL-IN. As a part of my program, she joined 4 years ago was weekly assignments and she did every single one and would post videos in the Facebook group sharing her breakthroughs and breakdowns. It was totally raw, powerful, pure faith… Keira. Over the years, I've watched her start her businesses, and continually expand who she is and how big she plays. When she joined my high-level coaching program, which isn't cheap, I was so excited! Then, like she did just like before, and went ALL-IN! She soaked it up like a sponge and transformed quickly and profoundly. I then watched her join some of the high-level groups that I am a part of, and she did the same thing… totally ALL-IN, no holding back, and utter and near immediate transformation. She never stops outgrowing herself, is always evolving and learning higher-level rules to create higher-level results and transformation for herself and those she fiercely and devotedly serves. I'm so glad she wrote this book; it's how I've seen her create the miracles and other amazing things she's done and will continue to do. With God, you can achieve the impossible. There are no limits. Listen to Keira, read this book. She's the best one to teach this concept."

-Dr. Benjamin Hardy, Organizational Psychologist
and Author of ***Be Your Future Self Now***
www.benjaminhardy.com

"Working with Keira Poulsen transformed my life – in less than a year I've published two books, been a contributing author in two books, and I'm working on two more that will be published soon. I've also created my business and podcast Evolving to Exceptional with multiple programs and courses, been a keynote speaker, and so much more! Keira's practices have transformed my life and allowed me to move through challenges, healing, and building my business so much faster than I ever could have on my own!"

-Jessica Tietjen, J.D., Author of
The Exceptional Life R-Evolution, Fiercely Cherished Beings,
and coauthor of ***Collaboration with the Divine.***
www.evolvingtoexceptional.com

"I have had my book inside of me for over four years. It would tap me on the shoulder from time to time to remind me that it was still there and waiting for me to be brave enough to write the words that were inside of me. One day, I looked out my rear window and although my career had helped me to attain all my financial dreams, I was completely unfulfilled. I realized that I wasn't using my spiritual gifts to help make an impact on the world. And then Keira was introduced to me. I knew immediately that she would be the one that could help me get out of my head and into my heart. Now after writing my book, writing courses, and producing an inspirational video, I can't help but tear up with my love and admiration for this beautiful woman who inspired and showed me tangible steps to step into the highest and best version of myself."

-Wendy Bunnel, Author of upcoming book,
Truth and Dare: Daring to Live Your Truth in a Fake World
www.wendybunnell.com

"Being in Keira's presence will light you up and change you. She's one of those powerful women, who once you have on your side, will support you and your business growing at light speed. She's not only committed to you, she's really a genius at what she does. AND she cares. Really cares. And that to me is priceless."

-Eia, Multidimensional Medicine Woman
www.medicinewomanrising.com

"Keira is more than a writing coach. She's more than a business coach. She is the type of leader you want to follow because she shows all the way up for herself and does the work, and then shows all the way up for you. I could not have written and published my book without her. I would not be where I am in expanding my business without her. She held my hand as I slayed my inner dragons of self-doubt, fear, and blocks that held me back from being all that I can be. She created a community of other entrepreneurs and heart-centered thought-leaders who are just as passionate about serving the world and supporting each other in being successful. In that community we have cried, laughed, collaborated, and created together. Keira has given me the support, strength, courage, and tools to build my dream career from a place of joy and gratitude. She has modeled how business can be done when I trust myself, trust in the Divine, and watch the miracles happen in my life."

-Julie Elizabeth,
Author of *Sacred Sexuality*
www.freedomhousepublishingco.com/meetjulieelizabeth

"I was seeking a mentor to help me write and share my message, and none of the mainstreaming marketing approaches resonated with me. They all seemed to mimic each other and although I told myself I *should* follow these strategies because they are what have made other authors very successful, my soul said, "keep looking." I was introduced to Keira by one of my mentors and from our first conversation, I felt at peace and excited to write my book! Being guided by Keira was perfect for me because she speaks and operates in my heart and soul language: living by divine guidance. I am so grateful that my first manuscript is finished and is being edited at this moment. She focused her coaching on what matters most, the connection of my mind, body, heart and soul with the Divine. As these elements aligned, writing just flowed and felt joyful."

-Angel Lyn, MSW, Soul Mentor,
Author of upcoming book, *Soul-u-lar Evolution:*
A Mormon Woman's Transcendent Journey to Love
and coauthor of *Collaboration with the Divine*
https://angel-naivalu-soul-mentor.business.site/

"Coaching with Keira has been one magical experience! When I first learned about her Mastermind, I felt like it was my next steps to take me and my coaching business to the next level. I was absolutely right! Keira has a way of teaching how to bring books, courses and your work through in the most incredible way! Since joining her mastermind I have received three new clients, began writing my book that will be published this year and I am putting together content for three online courses right now! If you are ready to take action and make your business happen in the most heart centered aligned way, this is your place!"

-Dana Parker,
Author of upcoming book, *Evolving Female Leaders*
www.innerworldmovement.com

"Working with Keira has allowed me to see parts of myself that I haven't recognized before. She shares her knowledge with great enthusiasm and love for all. What drew me to her is her genuine and authentic way of being in this world. Since working with her I've been inspired to show up in ways I have never done before. I dare to believe in myself and get out of my comfort zone! Recently I've just opened my own business, co-authored in a collaboration book and learning to truly embrace my gifts!"

-Valerie Bote, Coauthor of *Collaboration with the Divine*
www.lifeinmotionhealing.com

"Working with Keira not only expedited the completion of my book but helped me to create momentum in all other areas of my life. I joined Keira's Mastermind the beginning of December and was finished writing my book April 14th. This was the first book I've ever written. Keira's methods and processes are priceless in teaching the art of receiving revelation and abundance. Her natural gift is to unlock messages you didn't know were being stored in your body. There were instances just being around her and not even talking about books that I received downloads from the divine to write.

The energy of a group working towards a common goal was another aspect of being a part of the Mastermind that assisted me. The group all working towards a common goal of writing a book sped up the delivery of miracles and information as I worked on my book. If you're wanting expert guidance throughout writing your book alongside receiving the support you need, Keira is the coach for you! I'm so grateful for her commitment to restoring sacred writing one author at a time. I highly recommend her to anyone who tells me they're wanting to write a book."

-Lindsey Bryant, Author of *The High Priestess*
https://linktr.ee/lindseybryantboiseid

TABLE OF CONTENTS

INTRO

God is My Business Plan is a Sacred Revolution.

A revolution within business and creation.

It is time that we all rise up and awaken to our gifts of creation and being guided by the Divine.

This guidebook is designed to teach you a new way of creating and running a successful business.

Let this book invite you into the powerful world of creation, healing, and leading with light!

Welcome.

xo

Keira

CHAPTER 1

HOW IT ALL BEGAN

5 YEARS AGO, ON FEB 17TH, 2017, I HEARD GOD.

I heard God like I had never heard God before.

It was a powerful knowing: a truth that came to me in a time of deep pain and need.

I was deep in the pains of trauma memories surfacing and I wanted to leave this world. The pain was so intense, I just wanted out.

I felt completely deserted and alone.

With the pain and memories of being sexually abused as a child surfacing, I was angry with God. Angry that God had not protected little Keira. Angry that such horrific abuse happens to so many people. And I wanted out.

I wanted to leave this world.

A world where God didn't protect innocent little children from such terror and pain.

I decided that I was going to end my life.

It seemed at that moment the only solution I had left. The pain had expanded past my level of tolerance. And this was the only way out.

Until God stopped me.

I felt a presence surrounding my body, and a voice that said: "Stop. You have work to do."

And something deep inside of me agreed.

My face was covered in snot, my body exhausted from sobbing, and yet somewhere, something within me had agreed.

Not only did my higher-self agree to stay on this earth, but I made a commitment to God.

If I was going to stay here on this earth filled with trauma and pain, then God would have to show me WHY I was here.

And if God would show me, then I would do everything I was inspired to do.

From that day forward, this was the model of how I lived each day of my life.

Each inspiration that came, I took action.

It was my partnership with God.

Inspiration would flow, and I would act, even when it didn't make sense. I would act especially when I was afraid, doubted my abilities, and wanted to quit. It was in those moments that I would rise with extra power and act with unbridled faith.

ACTION WITH UNBRIDLED FAITH CREATES PATHWAYS OF MIRACLES.

The reason I was able to keep taking action, time after time, day after day—even in the face of fear, resistance, and massive self-doubt—was that ***this*** *was healing me.*

Each action I took healed a fragment of my broken self.

Each creation I brought to life activated my gifts and brought me into wholeness.

After spending years numbing on sugar and caffeine, living life overwhelmed and unhappy . . . I was finally becoming alive.

And what was bringing me to life was partnering with God.

I had no intention of starting a business; I just was committed to doing what God inspired me to do.

Each time I was inspired and then I acted . . . my life would change.

How did it change?

To really grasp the changes that have happened, I want to take you back to what life was like for me only 5 years ago.

I would spend most of my days doing laundry, watching 2 hours of t.v. during my baby's nap time, only to then pull my tired body off the couch and out to the car, then drive down to the gas station (every day) at 2:30 pm, and drag myself in through the heavy glass doors, where I would get my Dr. Pepper fix. By this time of the day, I was on my 2nd round of Dr. Pepper. And because I showed up each day with a baby on my hip and tired eyes, the employees would always wink at me and tell me that my drink was on them. Little did they know they were just helping me stay numb—numb to the life that was slowly killing me. A life that was being wasted by numbing out and disconnecting. I would then pick kids up from school, go home to do endless dishes, make dinner, and then massage my clients (a few nights a week).

I was drowning.

I thought I was drowning because I had 5 kids, house chores that never seemed to end—and it didn't feel like there would ever be an end in sight.

But the truth is: I wasn't drowning because of those things. I was drowning because I was living way BELOW my gifts, my abilities, and my purpose. My soul was drowning in the monotony of life.

I had no passion, no activities that lit me up. I made $12,00 a year (in a good year) and the saddest part was—I had forgotten how to dream.

Fast forward only 5 years and I still have 5 kids, mounds of laundry to do, endless dishes to be washed AND I run multiple businesses that cumulatively gross mutliple-6 figures. I own a publishing house that publishes books that are created to transform humanity, I run 2 masterminds, I have written 4 books, I host a podcast,

I drop daily prayer videos on YouTube, and I channel books with new authors Monday–Friday live on Instagram. I spend 2 hours a day in my sacred tent working with God and my angels. I take salsa dancing classes one night a week and I watch the sun rise each morning over the glorious mountains outside of my sacred tent.

Nothing has changed, and everything has changed.

I gave up my addiction to caffeine, let go of my emotional eating patterns that I had used to numb my pain, and released 35 pounds. I can honestly say that I added 100x *more* to my plate and I am happier than I have ever been.

How?

I PARTNERED WITH GOD.

God became my partner in life, my best business coach, and ultimately—God IS my Business Plan.

This book is what I have learned about business from God.

God also guided me to hire amazing business coaches, work with extraordinary therapists, and join powerful masterminds to support me on this path.

But I was guided to each one of them. I didn't choose them; they were chosen for me.

When each mentor came into my life, I knew that God had sent them. The signs were always there, reaffirming God's hand was clearing the path. I began to work with my angels and witnessed miracles happening every single time.

The success in business meant the success of my impact on the world. God wanted me to succeed in business because that meant MORE people would be impacted with the message I am here to share and the work I am here to do.

My work is to help people hear God.

That is my purpose, my desire, and my agreement.

And so, I have sprinted. I have worked hours upon hours; I have healed, created, written, and recorded—always with an open heart, a student mind, and a willingness to lean into the fear.

THE RESULT: I AM ALIVE.

And not only just the breathing, here-on-earth alive—*and I do celebrate daily that I chose to live.*

But the ALIVENESS that comes when you live your purpose, when you are guided by God, and when you create with a lava-intense energy.

I AM ALIVE.

This book is a guidebook. A place to unlearn what you think you know about business, rules, and success.

This book is the fire into which you throw all that hasn't worked for you, all that isn't working, and all the fears of failure. Then allow the ashes of this fire to be soil for new:

The new and brilliant YOU. The new partnership for you and God.

And the true work you are here on this earth to do.

God is My Business Plan will take you through healing practices, working with your angels, and most importantly—HOW to hear God.

Success is deeply important for those who are here to impact the world.

We need YOU to succeed. Because when you are successful, that means your message is thriving, alive, and serving humanity.

THE FIRST THING WE WILL DO TOGETHER ON THIS JOURNEY IS FOR YOU TO THROW EVERYTHING INTO THE FIRE.

And I mean a real fire.

You are going to do this practice with me right here and now.

You can watch the video I created for you on my BONUS page:

https://keira-poulsen.mykajabi.com/God Is My Business Plan BONUS

Or you can do this on your own.

THROWING YOUR CLOTHES IN THE FIRE

I am asking you to throw your clothes in the fire.

This is symbolic of course.

I'm not really asking you to strip down and burn your clothes. But I am asking you to burn all the beliefs that you have built up around business and God.

To begin, you will write out the beliefs that you are ready to let go of and burn.

You can't fill a bucket with water if it's already filled to the brim.

You need to empty out the contents inside of you so there is room for the new inspiration that will be coming to you through this book and through your own personal ability to receive from God.

To get you started, here are a few beliefs to write out that you might relate to:

1. I don't know how to hear God.

2. I'm not good enough for God to speak to me

3. I'm not holy or righteous enough

4. I don't believe in God

5. I suck at business

6. I always fail

7. No matter what I do, I can't seem to get ahead

8. I am tired of trying; everyone else seems to know what to do but me

9. How could God be my business partner?

10. I am not good enough

Write it ALL out: the lies, the beliefs, the old ways that no longer serve you.

THEN BURN THAT SHIT.

Burn it and watch each letter on the pages dissolve right before your eyes. They are leaving your body, your mind, and your cells.

LET IT LEAVE YOU NOW.

Take a deep breath in and as you breathe out, notice how you feel.

Can you feel that there is a bit more space within you?

THIS IS HOW WE START THIS BOOK.

With space.

It is within the spaces that you can receive the new.

Walk away from that fire *cleansed*.

The old has been burned and YOU are the Phoenix ready to rise in the NEW.

CHAPTER 2

LIFE BLOOD

Business + Spirituality are my LIFE BLOOD. It is my passion. This is what I go to sleep thinking about, this is what my brain chews on all day, this is what gives me my energy and excitement.

I believe that when we bring God INTO business with us, success is inevitable. When we can allow ourselves to be guided by, directed by, and received from God in regard to business—miracles will show up each day of your life.

This is NOT a religious book.

This is a spiritual book.

Anyone and everyone can believe in a higher Source that leads them, loves them, and inspires them to create and make a difference in the world.

For me, that is God, and my spiritual team.

But for you, it could be the Divine, Source, Love, or the Universe.

Choose what name fits best in your soul. What do you feel safest with? Use that word instead so that the message of this book fits for you.

I believe that if you have found this book, then you are a change-maker.

You are here to transform humanity with light.

You are here for a distinct reason and purpose.

And so, it is deeply important that you create success with your business. If you don't succeed in business, then you don't get to create and use your gifts as they were intended to do. Instead, you have to find a different job that will drain your energy, take up your time, and ultimately distract you from the powerful work you are here to do.

If you aren't successful in the business your soul wants to create, your energy will fizzle out, and eventually, you will quit, leaving a hole in your soul and depriving the world of the powerful work you were created to do.

But if you can be successful, then you will continue to grow in the creation of your work.

Many people will be blessed by your messages, your gifts, and the light you have to offer.

You will also see that your life and your family's life will be blessed as you grow and succeed in business.

It is a win-win every single time.

I have seen this in my own life.

I see it in my client's lives.

And I am ready to share with you that I have learned.

I believe that now, as the world is being cleansed of the old ways and we are being invited to live from new spaces, the world needs more leaders, creators, healers, authors, and Divinely guided business owners.

That is: **you.**

You are needed.

The work inside of you that is asking to be created and brought forward into the world is deeply needed.

I see you; I hold the space for you, and I believe that with the tools I teach you, you will have everything you need to be successful in all that you do.

I also understand that business is hard. It can be exhausting, overwhelming, and lonely.

You may be at the beginning of business, just starting out. Or you might be a few years in, have invested all the money you have and more, and feel like you are spinning and not sure how to get traction.

And you might be extremely successful at what you do and want to expand even further with more ease.

This book will meet you wherever you are.

In any place along your journey, these tools and practices will only elevate and quicken your results.

This book isn't a book. It is actually a guide. It will read like a guide because it is the course work to my most popular digital course. This guidebook is a business in a box and will guide you every step of the way.

Throughout these pages, I will teach you the action steps of what a business guided by the Divine looks like.

Imagine that this book is your **How-To Guide** on building a successful thought-leader business.

It is THE THING you have been looking for.

And if you allow yourself to swim in the river of spirituality with me, everything will become so much easier.

All that we do here in this book is guided by SERVICE—service to humanity.

Your *soul* purpose is here to serve; serve those who only YOU can reach.

You know that you have gifts inside of you that will make a difference.

You know that you are here to serve at the highest level.

And that is why it can be so frustrating when things don't work out, or when you get stuck.

Because this passion inside of you is so big, *you cannot ignore it.*

But this way is old, tiring and we are clearing it out of your life.

Business becomes easier . . . now.

When you learn how to create and work from a spiritual standpoint, everything gets easier.

Your creations will come together quicker.

Your mind will begin to understand what needs to happen and success will start to flow.

Welcome to a new way of thinking, creating, and leading.

CHAPTER 3

COMMITMENT TO THE WORK

This guidebook is here to support you in massive success. Success in ALL the areas of your life.

But there are many detours on the path of success. And so, we are going to create a safety structure for you.

Here is how:

1. You will learn how to clear out the old beliefs

2. Create Commitments to yourself and your work

3. Learn how to create a spiritual practice that becomes the hub of your work

4. Activate and UNBLOCK the CREATOR inside of you

5. Dive into the tactical practices of business

6. Awaken the healer within you

I have many videos, meditations and printable PDF's to support you in this guidebook.

All are available on the BONUS page here:

As you begin to create and pull yourself into new shapes, new mindsets, and new ways of being, your old patterns and belief systems will want to rear their heads. Fear and doubt will probably visit, and it will be easy to want to quit.

It is for this reason that most entrepreneurs fail.

They don't fail because their work isn't good, or because their programs don't work. They fail because they got stuck in their head. Fear and doubt destroyed them. And so, they quit.

But if you partner with God, create a sacred practice that allows you to heal your nervous system, connect to your SOUL and hear God- miracles will be the air in which you breathe in.

You will clear out the fear, the self-doubt, the parts inside of you that don't want to take action!

Simply put:

You will succeed:

- When your creations are being guided by The Divine

- When you are doing daily healing work on the obstacles that show up

- When you know the practical and basic steps needed to run a business

- When you allow yourself to fully show up in your gifts as the leader and lightworker that you are

These are the tools you need to be successful as a thought-leader, a creator, a writer, a healer, and a teacher.

All that is required of you to listen to Divine inspiration and take action.

I can teach you how to get there, but I cannot make you walk.

MY PROMISE TO YOU:

I promise to show up 100% for you in this book.

I promise to teach you all that I know in the realm of Spiritual Entrepreneurship.

I promise to hold the space for you and your success.

This is my declaration to YOU.

I ask that you create your own promise and declaration to yourself.

Grab a piece of paper and write down this declaration.

"I, (insert your name here,) make a promise to myself and to my work that I will show up FULLY as I read through this guidebook. I have a clear mind, and a hopeful heart. I commit to taking the actions that are required for my work to succeed. I commit to my soul work (insert your work/ your passion/ your purpose here).

I honor my gifts; I bless my work and commit to being the leader of light that I am for myself and those around me. I am here for a purpose. I have been called to fill a role that only I can fill. I believe in myself because I am merely a vessel for light to be brought to this earth."

You can download this image on the BONUS page here: https://keira-poulsen.mykajabi.com/GodIsMyBusinessPlanBONUS

Or… you can use the next page to write your declaration in.

My Commitment

Date:

I am a leader of light
I am here to make a massive difference in the world
I commit to my purpose and devote myself to the creations I have been inspired to create

"I, "Insert your name here" make a promise to myself, and to my work that I will show up FULLY as I read through these chapters. I have a clear mind, and a hopeful heart. I commit to taking the actions that are required for my work to succeed. I commit to my soul work of "insert your work/ your passion/ your purpose here." I honor my gifts; I bless my work and commit to being the leader of light that I am for myself and those around me. I am here for a purpose. I have been called to fill a role that only I can fill. I believe in myself because I am merely a vessel for light to be brought to this earth."

MY COMMITMENT:

Place this declaration where you can read it multiple times a day.

Allow these words to be new seeds planted within your cells.

This is a new way.

I know you have tried many ways before to create success. I know the struggle, the burnout and the exhaustion tied to your effort. This guidebook is here to show you a different way.

But, before I can teach you what I have learned, we must clean out the old.

You don't want to embark on this new journey with old, beaten-down shoes that no longer fit.

You want fresh new shoes, ready to walk up the mountain.

To clear out the old, I invite you to set aside some time right now, to write out all of the old thought patterns around business and creation.

Here are some questions to ask yourself and to journal around:

- Am I afraid to let God be my business partner?

_____

_____

_____

_____

_____

- What has happened in the past when I tried to create or launch offerings?

_____

_____

_____

_____

_____

- If they did not go as well as I wanted them to, am I afraid that they will happen again?

_____

_____

_____

_____

- What limitations do I have that are already showing up, telling me that I will fail?

_____

_____

_____

_____

- What do I tell myself in regard to finishing projects?

_____

_____

_____

_____

- What bad experiences have I had connected to creating offerings, writing my book, sharing my messages through social media, gathering clients, selling my offerings, etc.

_____

_____

_____

_____

- What is my deepest fear about being successful?

_____

_____

_____

_____

_____

- Do I resist success? If so, why?

_____

_____

_____

_____

_____

- What are my fears of failing?

_____

_____

_____

_____

_____

- And is there anything else that is currently blocking me from truly succeeding in business?

_____

_____

_____

_____

CLEAR OUT THE OLD

We don't want to embark on this new journey with the beaten down shoes that's already on. We want fresh new shoes, ready to walk up the mountain.
Let's Clear Out The OLD.

- Am I afraid to let God be my business partner?
- What has happened in the past when I tried to create or launch offerings?
- If they did not go as well as I wanted them to, am I afraid that they will happen again?
- What limitations do I have that are already showing up telling me that I will fail?
- What do I tell myself in regard to finishing projects?
- What bad experiences have I had connected to creating offerings, writing my book, sharing my messages through social media, gathering clients, selling my offerings, etc.
- What is my deepest fear about being successful?
- Do I resist success? If so, why?
- What are my fears of failing?
- Is there anything else that is currently blocking you from truly succeeding in this program.

Once you have written everything out, I want you to take this paper to a fire-safe place and burn it.

As these words burn and are turned into ashes, I invite you to truly allow them all to leave. When all that is left are ashes, take a deep cleansing breath in and blow them away.

I want you to physically feel the release of these words, these past emotions, and the experiences as they dissipate.

You are now free.

Free of the past.

Now it is time for you to begin.

Start fresh; start new as the successful leader and creator that you are!

CHAPTER 4

HOW I CAN SUPPORT YOU

I have a few magical gifts that allow me to serve humanity. The three most magical ones are:

1. Helping people hear God

2. Channeling books with authors so they can write THE book that is in their heart—quickly

3. UNBLOCKING CREATORS

HERE ARE SOME WAYS I CAN SUPPORT YOU IN THESE 3 AREAS:

THIS GUIDEBOOK:

My intention with this guidebook is to help you strengthen your "receiving muscle." I have dedicated this guidebook to support you in opening up your own abilities of receiving so that you can hear God, *for you and create from that powerful source of light.*

BOOK CHANNELING:

If you want to channel your book with me, I do this LIVE, Monday–Friday on my Instagram: @keirapoulsen. You can sign up to do a live book channeling with me by clicking here:

https://app.acuityscheduling.com/schedule.php?owner=20041183&appointmentType=21688832

Or you can just click the link in my Instagram bio to access my calendar link: @keirapoulsen.

I also run a mastermind for men and women who are ready to channel their books and publish them in 6 months or less!! You can learn more about this mastermind on the BONUS page.

https://keira-poulsen.mykajabi.com/GodIsMyBusinessPlanBONUS

UNBLOCKING THE CREATOR:

This is happening everywhere.

When you spend time with me in my podcast, YouTube videos, channel LIVE with me on Instagram, join my mastermind, or become a Freedom House author- you will experience THIS.

The focus in all that I do is to unblock the creator inside of each human that I come in contact with.

Why?

Because it is the MAGIC of life.

When your creator is unblocked, your ability to receive, create, and take action is heightened.

This is where YOU become alive.

Creation heals you.

It is the sword that clears out the clutter in your mind, and the fire that helps you MOVE!

Creation that is connected to receiving from God is the ultimate expression of joy and expression.

So today, right here, right now- we are going to UNBLOCK the CREATOR INSIDE YOU!

I am going to walk you through a visualization. You can do it with me in video form on my BONUS page **here:**

https://keira-poulsen.mykajabi.com/GodIsMyBusinessPlanBONUS or read through the practice below.

Are You Ready?

Let's Unblock Your Creator....

To begin, lie down in a safe place.

Make sure you have a warm blanket to wrap yourself in, and that you can be alone for the next 10 minutes.

Come back to your breath. Notice it, feel it, and welcome it in.

Take a deep breath all the way down to your lower belly. Expanding your lungs to full capacity, allow the breath to move into any tightness in your ribs.

Now return to your normal breathing as we begin to bring in the warmth of the sun to soften your heart. Allow the warmth of the sun to peel back any layers that you may have. Softening the debris, the walls and the locks around your heart.

Slowly push yourself to the side and roll up to a sitting position.

Keeping your eyes closed, I want you to imagine that I am sitting here with you. I am going to gather your hands in my hands, facing you knee to knee, we just sit here in this warmth and light.

As I sit here with you, I invite you to share with me all that you are doing "wrong". Tell me why the creations aren't working. Share with me why you are stuck. Speak these things out loud. Let them rise up from the corners they have been tucked away in.

They will most likely have a tint of shame or doubt tied to them. They won't feel good to say and yet, they need to leave your body.

As you share with me, know that I am here to witness. I am holding the space for you.

What are the pieces that you don't like about yourself? What tendencies, weaknesses and darkness do you have inside of your body and your life that you hide, ignore and push away?

Bring them here.

And know that as you share them, I only see the light. I only see how they have been your magic.

The darkness, the pain, the things you HATE about yourself *have created the fire that got you HERE.*

They aren't to be shamed or ignored.

They are meant to breathe oxygen. They are meant to be witnessed.

They are here to be loved.

As you bring them here to sit with us, we get to acknowledge them for the critical role they have played in your life.

Now, if you are comfortable with this, I am going to move over and let God sit here with you. I want you to imagine God holding your hands and showing you why He loves these pieces about you.

Keep your heart open.

Allow your intuitive gifts to pull a seat up and help you see.

Ask God to show you why these dark parts, that have been shamed, hated and stuffed away are worthy of love.

Ask to see the magic in the hell.

And then witness.

You may hear, see, feel or simply know.

Trust this process.

It will work.

As you begin to witness the miracles and the magic of your pain and struggles, I want to bring you to the awareness of the warmth in your arms.

God's love is pouring out from his heart through his arms to you. This love begins to radiate warmth through your hands, up your arms and into your heart.

Take a deep breath in and allow the love in.

You can say in your heart or in your mind:

"I open up to receive this love. I am allowed to be **this** loved. I welcome this love. I am grateful for this love. Please help me to stay open so I can receive the love that is here for me."

Notice that your body is vibrating with this warmth and love. The dark corners have now been filled with this glorious nectar.

Each broken space has been seamed together with love. And you begin to feel some energy moving in your lower belly.

Bring this love here.

The love that has been flowing in your heart is now moving down through your body and gently nestles into your lower belly, *the sacral chakra.*

A warmth begins to expand through your lower belly, and **creation unfolds.**

Ask God, "What creation is wanting to come through you right now?"

What is the creation that is bursting to come through you?

See it, feel it, know it.

It is here for YOU.

As you dance with this creation, you will be wrapped in momentum and joy.

This creation is a gift.

A gift for you.

Breathe it in and feel it ebb and flow throughout your body. *Witness the magic that is here.*

The magic of creation with the Divine.

Allow yourself to smile, to giggle or to simply feel at peace.

This creation has been unblocked and awakened.

But it needs your body to fully birth to this reality. And so, it requires action on your part.

Ask God to show you, *what is the first action step needed for this creation to come to life?*

Drop out of the mind and into the heart.

And listen.

Listen with your spiritual gifts of seeing, hearing, feeling and knowing.

Witness as the answer is dropped in.

And it will.

Because when we ask... we receive.

Take a nice deep breath in and feel the warmth radiating throughout your entire being.

You are fully alive in this love.

The love for ALL of you.

You may feel tingling move through your body. Breathe that in. This is the magic that occurs when we unblock our creator.

Bring your presence back to God and know that at any time you can come and sit here with God.

I began this practice with you to support you. But I am not needed. I was the bridge to begin the process of feeling at ease, at peace and safe.

From here on out, you can do this practice by calling in God right away. Allow God to hold your broken pieces and remind you how loved they are.

Allow the love to unblock the creator within.

Take a deep breath in and audibly release your breath.

We have unblocked the creator within you, and now we step forward into action.

Creation is a VERB.

It is the magic of energy and action.

To do this we are going to call in our board of directors. Our spiritual team is here to participate when we call upon them.

Invite your angels, your guides and your spiritual team to help you take the action step that you just received from God.

Today.

Don't put it off.

The creator within you is unblocked. Use this opportunity to CREATE!

And when that action step has been completed, come back into your heart and ASK for the next step.

Taking guided action, one step at a time is how we play in the realm of creation and miracles.

Are you READYYYYYYYY??

Let's start with the most important and impactful FIRST step.

SACRED SPACE

CHAPTER 5

SACRED SPACE

Creating a Sacred Space, and having a Sacred Space Practice, are essential to your success. This is vital and of the most importance.

A Sacred Space Practice is where you will go to be guided by The Divine and work with your spiritual team. This is the cornerstone of all that we will be doing in this guidebook.

If you would like support in creating your very own Sacred Space Practice, I have a YouTube series called, "God is My Business Plan," where I lead you in morning and evening videos to help you create this practice. You can find a link to these videos on my BONUS page:

https://keira-poulsen.mykajabi.com/GodIsMyBusinessPlanBONUS

This chapter is dedicated to teaching you how to create our own Sacred Space Practice.

HOW TO CREATE YOUR SACRED SPACE:

There are a few steps in the creation and dedication of a sacred space. Once you have located and dedicated your sacred space to be a place of connection between you, God, and your spiritual team, it will become a place of refuge and receiving.

STEP 1: FIND THE SACRED SPACE

Ask God to show you where your sacred space is. You will start by putting out the request to know where your sacred space is, right before you fall asleep. Just like

Thomas Edison taught: "Never go to sleep without a request to your subconscious." That is the principle that we are using here and now. But we are going to put the request up to God. When your head hits the pillow and you are about to fall asleep, you are going to send up the request that you will be shown where in your home you can create a sacred space. Ask to be shown it in your sleep or right when you wake up. Then allow yourself to receive. This might take one day or a few days but keep asking. You will receive. Then allow God to show it to you during the following day. Keep an open mind, attached to nothing. Let go of where you think it should be, and instead allow it to be shown to you.

You will notice that while you are walking around your house, a spot will jump out at you! It might be a closet that no one uses, or a corner in your bedroom. Maybe you decide to purchase a tent like I have and that will place it in your backyard.

Ideas will come; let them in and trust that you ARE being guided.

Once you have located a Sacred Space, then you can move onto Step 2.

Step one is complete.

STEP 2: CLEAN AND CLEAR THE ENERGY OF THE SACRED SPACE.

> *I work with the Ascended Master, Christ, when I heal and cleanse space. If that resonates with you, follow along. If that doesn't, you can always ask "the Divine Light" to clear the space.*

I first start by asking that Christ will touch the walls, the floors, the doors, the windows, and anything and everything that is within the space. I ask that as Christ touches each location in the room, it will be cleansed and cleaned; that anything that is not light and that is not at the vibrational frequency of miracles and light be cleaned out completely. I then ask that Christ will activate the frequency of the space to be at the level of miracles and Divine Light. You can then dedicate this space for the intention of your sacred work. You can speak out loud something like this:

> *"I dedicate this space to my sacred work, for receiving, and for the intention of creating with the Divine."*

Speak out loud what intention you are putting into this space.

Step 2 is now complete.

STEP 3: CALL IN YOUR SPIRITUAL TEAM

Every time you come to your sacred space; you will call in your spiritual team. But for this first "set-up" time, you will call them in and give them assignments.

Here is an example you can follow. Feel free to tweak it and make it your own.

> *"I call in all of my angels and spiritual team—those who are here to lead me, guide me, direct my work and my mission, in and through the Divine Light. I ask you to support this sacred space and hold it in safety for me. I ask that this space may be a refuge and a place of Divine receiving. Thank you, thank you, thank you."*

Step 3 is now complete.

STEP 4: FILL IT WITH YOUR LOVE.

This step is fun and delicious. I want you to start to put things into this space that you love. Do you love paintings, art, crystals, warm blankets, etc.? Start to allow your heart to choose what goes in your sacred space. Even if your sacred space is a tiny spot on the floor in your living room, you can have a basket of your favorite items to pull out each time you create a sacred space.

Get creative, play, and enjoy!

Step 4 is complete.

STEP 5: MAKE THE TIME TO BE IN SACRED SPACE.

The final step is to GO to your sacred space! I suggest going every morning and every evening. Even if it is for only 10 minutes each time, your life will change. When you can spend time in this dedicated space, your energy will shift! Your life will expand as you create in a place of high vibrational frequency and open up to receive.

Step 5 is complete.

CHAPTER 6

WORKING WITH
YOUR SPIRITUAL TEAM

Working with my Spiritual Team is the most effective tool I use. I believe in the power of accessing my Spiritual Team to help me create my work, to help me find the clients who need my help, and to help me in many other aspects of my business and life.

Working with your Spiritual Team will help you in creating, in promoting, in solving problems, and in many other ways.

There is a level of support and guidance that comes when we rely on our Spiritual Team. As you grow more confident in working with your Spiritual Team, you will feel a deep level of love, support, and ease flow into your life. If this idea is new to you, then I invite you to simply experiment with this idea. Decide to just try it out and *begin to watch the miracles happen.*

I was working with a client who was burned out and tired. She was doing ALL the things in her business and it was draining her, *(sound familiar)* because this is how MOST entrepreneurs feel. We were doing some healing work on her nervous system when I was shown a vision. I am going to walk you through this, because it will land deeper in your body if I share it with you, instead of teaching you.

Imagine that you invited your best friends over to your house for a big dinner party. You invite them to sit at your table while you cook. You have five dishes that you are working on and it is not easy. The kitchen is hot, you are sweating, kids are running around your legs and clearly you need help. Your friends keep offering to help, but you assure them that you can do it!! They sit there, watching you work endlessly, on your own.

Now imagine if YOU were one of those friends. It would be impossible to JUST sit there and watch!!

This is how your angels are feeling towards you!

They are surrounding you with love, just WAITING for you to ask them to help.

They live within the law and boundaries of agency. Which means-you must ASK for them to fully participate in your life.

But once you ask, they are 100% on board! *Grateful and joyful to be in the work with you.*

Imagine the sweet joy you would feel helping out your friend. Maybe you hold her baby while she bakes the cookies. Or maybe you run to the grocery store to pick up the one item she forgot.

Whatever she needs, you would step up and help.

This is how your angels can be for you! Ask them to support you in ALL the things. Work, kids, dinner, finances, clients, relationships, problems that need solved.... You name it and they are there for you!

When you ask....

As Spiritual Entrepreneurs, our lives are greatly supported by our angels and our guides. Your work is important in this world. It is my belief that you have an army of angels here to lead, guide, and support you. Enjoy experimenting with this idea!

I invite you to take a few moments today and experiment with calling in your Spiritual Team. Allow your inner trust and surrender to pave a pathway for miracles and support to happen.

ACTION STEPS:

Use the words on the next page to practice calling in your Spiritual Team. Take a few moments today to use this tool. As you use it more, you will see the results flow in. *Remember* My words are not the right words. They are just templates. Use the words that feel good to you!

Also... I LOVE to hear these stories. They are my FAVVVV thing ever!!

Feel free to DM me on Instagram @keirapoulsen to share your stories!

Spiritual Team

Receive SUPPORT + LOVE + MIRACLES

I call in my board of directors:

My angels,

Those who have been assigned to my work,

Those who are here to lead me, direct me, heal me, and guide me,

Those who have wisdom and experience to support my soul work, my message and my purpose.

I invite them to be here to support me, in and through the Divine Light.

CHAPTER 7

THE SACRED
CREATIVE PROCESS

This is THE magic. The Sacred Creative Process is designed to support creatives, writers, podcasters, thought leaders, and entrepreneurs in every aspect of their lives.

Everyone loves to be in flow. FLOW is the coveted energetic space for everyone. When you are in flow, magic happens. You can write a digital course, a book, a podcast, a social media post—quickly and easily!

But flow can feel like the mirage that only shows up when it wants to.

Until now . . .

I have found a process that triggers your mind, body, and spirit into FLOW state at ANY time and in ANY place.

The Sacred Creative Process is the trigger that will pull you out of your mind and drop you into your heart.

To begin, I will be teaching you WHY each step is important and HOW it works.

Step 1: You will begin the Sacred Creative Process with the sense of smell.

WHY? Because smell triggers memories.

You will use your sense of smell at the beginning to train your brain to know when you are opening up to receive or channel your writing.

Pick an essential oil smell that you only use for this purpose so you can trigger automatic receiving at any time. You want to pick a smell that you love, that makes you feel good and that you ONLY use when you use The Sacred Creative Process.

Keeping this oil specific to this practice will help train your brain and your body to know when you are dropping into the flow and receiving state.

ACTIVATE WITH SMELL:

To begin, you will put a few drops of your chosen essential oil into your palms. Rub your hands together and then take a few breaths in. Allow the smell to move through your mind, your body and awaken your soul.

Step 2: Clear Your Energy Field

Just suppose that you went to the sink with your coffee mug that was filled with dirt and you put water in it. The water would become muddy. You wouldn't drink that water. Instead, you would clean out the coffee mug until the mug could hold clean water.

You are the coffee mug.

When you open up to receive and get into flow state, you want your energy to be clean to receive ideas, the visions, the words and the creation coming through you.

CLEAR YOUR ENERGY:

Imagine a brilliant white light above the top of your head.

Take a deep breath in and allow the light to come in through the crown of your head.

Visualize this light moving and ebbing through your body.

Invite the light to clean out any energy that isn't yours, that isn't serving you and that is blocking your receptivity.

Take another breath in and allow the light to activate all of your gifts. The light is the activator for your gifts.

Take a third breath in and allow the light to move all the way down to your toes. Direct the light to move out of your toes and create a beautiful shield of light around your whole body, sealing it back up at your toes.

Step 3: Calling in Your Spiritual Team

Studies show that 8 out of 10 of Americans believe in angels.

There is most likely a portion of you who don't . . .

Which is ok.

You don't have to understand this for it to work.

You just get to experiment with it.

You don't have to understand how electricity works to make the lights turn on in a room.

You just need to flip the light switch.

But, because the light turns on each time you flip the switch, you now trust the process.

The same applies to this step here.

You will use the process that we went through in chapter 6.

Remember- my words are a template. Say what feels right to you. But here is what I say:

WORKING WITH YOUR SPIRITUAL TEAM:

"I call in my spiritual team of angels. Those who have been assigned to me and my work. Those who are here to lead, direct, heal and guide me. Those who have wisdom and experience to support my soul work, my message and my purpose."

Step 4: Give Assignments to Your Team

Just like you give your assistant assignments to support your workflow, we are going to give your Spiritual Team assignments to support your channeling and for you to receive.

You will **ask for what you need from your Spiritual Team to support your work.**

If you are writing a book, ask them to help you find the time to write, clear the noise in your mind and receive the message easier.

If you are creating content, ask them to help you receive impactful ideas.

The list goes on and on.

Example:

If you are wanting help with creating a logo, here is what you could say:

> *"Angels, can you help me see the logo that would best serve my business? I would like this logo to call in and attract the perfect customers to my work. I want my customers to feel (insert emotion here) and I need the logo to express that feeling.*
>
> *Can you also show me the perfect designer for this logo? I would like to spend (insert the amount of money you want to spend) on this project. Can you bring me the designer who can create the perfect logo for that price?*
>
> *I need this logo complete by (insert the date you are desiring). Can you support me in this project? Thank you, thank you, thank you.*

GIVING OUT ASSIGNMENTS:

What are you creating right now?

What do you need help within your work?

Get very clear on the support you need and then begin to ask your spiritual team to accomplish those needs.

Step 5: The FINAL step: Prepare the Body to channel with the Prayer of Light.

This is simple, easy, and takes only 20 seconds.

Yet, it is the most profound step, because it will clear up ALL writer's block, confusion, and wasted time.

This Prayer of Light is something I say before I create, speak, coach, or write. This is how I access the Light and how I access clear and clean inspiration. There is power in our words, and I believe each time I say these words, the energy within me shifts. As I say this Prayer of Light, my human tendencies slip away, and I am able to really show up as a vessel for the work that needs to come through.

Before I started this practice, I would always mentally shame myself after every post I made, every podcast interview, heck- it was really anytime I shared. It was heavy to always feel so much shame when I chose to share.

But this Prayer of Light came to me in a time of need. I was asking God to show me how to share more in alignment with my gifts and to stop stumbling over my words. Most of all, I wanted to stop shaming myself each time I chose to share.

I was reading in the scriptures, and there was a part where Isaiah was preparing to meet with God and a similar practice was put into place. It stuck out to me so strongly and I knew I needed to implement this practice.

Since I have started using this tool, I never leave a situation where I second-guess what I said. Each word that comes from my mouth or that I write comes *through* me but not *from* me.

There is a difference here. Before, what I shared came FROM me. This prayer allows it to come THROUGH me instead.

I want you to start practicing with these words. Say them before you speak, write, or create. Allow them to cleanse the old and make way for the new.

PRAYER OF LIGHT:

I ask that the Divine Light will clean and cleanse my ears so that I may hear what needs to be heard.

I ask that Divine Light will clean my third eye so that I may have access to all of my spiritual gifts of seeing, hearing, feeling and knowing.

I ask that Divine Light will touch my lips so that they may be cleansed and cleared so that I may speak what needs to be spoken.

You have now gone through all 5 steps of The Sacred Creative Process.

If you would like to go through this process with me in video from, you can gain access to it on the BONUS page:
https://keira-poulsen.mykajabi.com/GodIsMyBusinessPlanBONUS

ACTION STEPS:

Use the Sacred Creative Process each time you create this week!!

CHAPTER 8

BE A VESSEL OF LIGHT

As we choose to step up and allow ourselves to be leaders, we are also being invited to bring light into the world.

This is very important for our work. This concept is very helpful when dealing with self-doubt, inadequacies, and fear. If you create your own content, your own ideas, and your own messages, then it is easy to doubt yourself. It is easy to doubt what you are creating. It is easy to feel inadequate.

But if you choose to allow the Divine to pour through you, your ideas, your creations, your insights, and your messages, then you are being a Vessel of Light. There is no reason to ever doubt what you create because you are simply being a vessel through which light came to this earth.

As you prepare your podcasts (either host or guest), if you allow your mind to take a backseat and step up your spiritual reception, your words will come out clean, clear, and powerful.

As you sit down to write a book, social media content, marketing material, articles, record a video; feeling into this idea, that you ARE a vessel of light; will change EVERYTHING.

When you allow yourself to be a vessel for light to come through you, then the words you write and the words you say, will come in clean and powerful.

The same is true for anything you create.

Handing over the need to "know it all" or "have it all figured out" will only enhance your ability to bring forward light to this world. Simply surrendering the control and need to have it all perfect is liberating, and **liberation is the energy of success.**

Feeling liberated in your creation, promotion, and work will bring in the feelings of ease and joy. Allow this idea to take a burden off your shoulders. Let this new belief help you surrender the human tendencies to "have it all under control," and then let the miraculous energies of liberation take place!

ACTION STEPS:

- Take time to do the "Vessel Of Light" Meditation: https://keira-poulsen.mykajabi.com/GodIsMyBusinessPlanBONUS

- Sit down and journal after the meditation

- Go through the questions below and journal what comes through

  o What reasons have I given myself to convince me that I am not qualified enough to share this message, write this book, be successful in my work, etc.?

  _____

  _____

  _____

  _____

  o Are these reasons true if I choose to be a Vessel of Light and allow the work to come through me?

  _____

  _____

  _____

  _____

o Am I willing to let go of the misconception that tells me I have to be qualified, certified, educated, healed, or anything else to be successful in my message and my work?

_____

_____

_____

_____

o Can I stand in the truth that **my life and my experiences qualify me for this work**?

_____

_____

_____

_____

o What is possible for me and for my work if I choose to create as a Vessel of Light?

_____

_____

_____

_____

In all of the creations, coaching, writing, podcasting, speaking, product design etc. that you do this week, I invite you to imagine being a Vessel of Light and allow for ideas and insights to flow through you!

CHAPTER 9

CREATING YOUR
WORK OF LIGHT

One of the greatest distractions and obstacles that gets in the way of creation is the culmination all of the things other people and programs have told you that you need to create.

This is messy. This is not how we work when God is our business plan! Instead, we allow ourselves to be guided, directed and we open up to receive insights, every day!

Today's chapter will help you get quiet so that you can receive whatever it is that the Divine would inspire you to create. As you do this, your creations will be more powerful, joyful, and successful!

There aren't many rules in spiritual entrepreneurship, but there is one I stick by, over and over.

This rule is that you NEVER create an offering that you feel like you "SHOULD" create.

Whenever a client comes to me and tells me that they "should" write a book or they "should" create a course, I stop them right away. No offering will succeed from the energy of "should." That energy is dead. It is forced. And good luck finding the excitement and joy you need when you have to sell something you thought you "should" create.

Everything you create needs to come from a desire—a desire that burns so brightly, it hurts to keep it inside. Those are the offerings that you will sell all day, every day because they LIGHT YOU UP.

I understand that there might have been a lot of outside influence that has been directing your work up till now, and that gets messy. When we listen to outside influence on what we should offer, we quiet our inner voice and are left agitated with poor results. Everything you create while in this book will be solely driven from the insights and inspiration you are receiving from the Divine.

Why?

Because the Divine KNOWS you.

God KNOWS your gifts and your purpose. So, the way I see it, let's ask the Source what you are here to create. When you do that, your creations will be the center and the seed of your joy and your service.

So, how do we begin? If you were in my Mentorship Program or my Mastermind, I would sit down and go through some questions.

Let's pretend we're sitting on the ground of my office, answering these questions and creating your Spiritual Business Outline.

- Who do YOU WANT to BE in the world?

_____

_____

_____

_____

- What visions do you have for your work? *(think Oprah level)*

_____

_____

_____

- What are the messages and the work you feel called to do?

  _____

  _____

  _____

- What creations and dreams do you have?

  _____

  _____

  _____

- What problem in the world does your service or message help or solve?

  _____

  _____

  _____

- What gifts do you have that can help you share this message or service with the world?

  _____

  _____

  _____

- Why do you feel so passionately about your purpose?

  _____

  _____

  _____

  _____

If you're having trouble answering these questions, here are two hints that might help.

Hint #1: I want you to think about what you are really good at. What comes so naturally to you that it seems silly to teach it to others? THIS is your gift. What comes to you with ease is what you are here to teach.

Hint #2: What are some ideas that have been flowing into your mind that seem impossible or scary? THIS is what you are being asked to create!

If it doesn't SCARE you and you don't feel nervous about what you are creating, then **dream bigger**! Playing small does not serve anyone.

Hiding your gifts takes more energy than sharing them with others.

Dreaming and creating big allows you to serve **bigger**.

CHAPTER 10

FUTURE SELF

I want you to sit for a few minutes and listen to the "Future Self Meditation" on the BONUS page here:

https://keira-poulsen.mykajabi.com/GodIsMyBusinessPlanBONUS

Once you listen to this meditation, I invite you to begin to write down all that you envision.

- Who are you here to become?

_____

_____

_____

_____

_____

- What will you be doing?

_____

_____

_____

_____

_____

- What will you have accomplished?

_____

_____

_____

_____

_____

- Who will you be serving?

_____

_____

_____

_____

_____

- What will your life look like?

_____

_____

_____

_____

_____

Get detailed. DREAM BIG. Enjoy this form of playing. When you deeply create and feel it to be true, you can really create this future self. This new future will unfold before your eyes. There is power in our words.

In the words of my favorite author, Florence Scovel Shinn, "Your words are your magic wand." And this statement could not be any truer.

What you say and think are the seeds for the life you live.

So, as we are in deep creation of your work, it is very important to keep your wording in the realm of "right now."

If you were to create from language like, "I am *going to be* a successful leader and podcaster in the healing world," the power that is available is missing. This type of language denotes that you are NOT all of these things now. And the **subconscious works in the here and now.** We want to make sure we speak as though it is true HERE and NOW. When we can do that, our subconscious will begin to create it here and now.

The normal way that people speak would be something like: *"I want* to be a successful business owner."

Instead, say something like, *"I am* a successful business owner."

Can you feel the difference?

There is a rooted energy about the second one.

It is tangible and REAL.

PLAY WITH THIS!

Feel the difference in your body when you speak in the "here and now" language. Write it as it is *right now*. Fill in the blanks. Make a few copies of this and allow yourself the gift of writing the "here and now."

I invite you to take all the dreams and creations that you saw in the Future Self meditation and write them out in the "here and now."

There is no more time to wait.

Waiting is a prison. There is never a perfect time. There is only: *now*.

The world needs your work. There are people who are seeking what you have to give. So, let's get the energy rolling in their direction.

By speaking your creations into the "here and now" template, you are allowing the energy for these dreams to become real.

Create your own mantras and speak them daily. Speak them into creation! I have listed some below (under Mantras) to give you a head start on your own mantra creation.

You and I know that you are here to create something special. I know you can feel it in your soul. That is what has led you here to me and to this book. Allow each one of these exercises to be guided by the Divine and your Inner Voice.

Allow new ideas—big ideas—unstoppable ideas to come forward. See them like new friends.

Welcome them into your world with open arms and a receiving heart.

You are a leader of light.

You are here with specific gifts that *only you have.*

Your mission and your purpose will ignite the light in others.

You are needed right here and right now.

Step forward and BE.

ACTION STEPS:

- Listen to the Future Self Meditation https://keira-poulsen.mykajabi.com/GodIsMyBusinessPlanBONUS

- Go through each of the following images in your sacred space.

- Allow yourself to receive ideas, inspiration, and visions.

Be My Future Self

Date:

WHO I ALREADY AM:

I am already:

My income is already:

My business is already:

YOU ARE YOUR MOST BRILLIANT SELF

I already FEEL:

I am ALREADY MY FUTURE BRILLIANT SELF.

This has ALL be done, under grace and in perfect ways.

MANTRAS

I am deeply grateful for my support team: my angels and guides. They open the pathways for miracles to occur.
Thank you, thank you, thank you.

I am a successful business owner. I always receive insights and solutions and I create with momentum. I always have amazing clients and customers who receive extraordinary results.
Thank you, thank you, thank you.

I am a brilliant creator. I create
with ease and am always guided by God.
Inspiration flows through me with ease and I
create with joy!
Thank you, thank you, thank you.

I am a published author. I received my book
with clarity, guidance, and ease. It awakened
my gifts and serves humanity at extraordinary
levels. I love being a published author. I love
sharing myself with the world. I love watching
people's lives change because of this work.
Thank you, thank you, thank you.

I am deeply happy. I see the magic of life all around me. Each day is filled with wonder and miracles. With each step I take, light ripples through me. I am whole. I am healed.
I am JOY.
Thank you, thank you, thank you.

I hear God. I speak with God. I am seen, held and witnessed. Divine love encircles me and holds me in safety and peace. I am perfect, just as I am.
Thank you, thank you, thank you.

CHAPTER 11

ALTAR TOOL

This tool is one of the most effective tools when it comes to carrying a lot of different creations and life at once. If you have ever felt overwhelmed by parenthood, life, bills, cleaning, AND creating as a leader, then this tool WILL change the way you experience life.

What if you had your own personal coach each morning to guide you on how your day will go? What if you had a coach show you the most important things to focus on for your business, your book, your mothering, your marriage, and any other relationships? Would it feel as though you were totally supported and at ease?

This is what altar work can do for you. God is the best business coach, guide, and time manager out there!

But what IS an altar?

I am not suggesting that you go out and buy a wooden altar for this practice.

No, this is a spiritual image that you see in your mind's eye. It is located between your heart and God's heart.

It is an altar because this is where you lay down your struggles. This is a place to put your worries, concerns or burdens and receive answers and guidance regarding them.

To do this practice for success in your work, you simply take one section of your business that you are needing guidance or inspiration with and lay it on the altar.

It is a full act of surrendering and trust.

Ask God to show you 1-3 ideas, inspiration and actions you can take regarding what you placed on the altar.

Ideas will come. And when they do, I want you to dedicate a notebook to the inspiration you are receiving. This book will be your Altar Work Notebook.

Write down what you hear, see and feel.

Spiritual inspiration leaves as quickly as it comes. You must bring it to earth by recording it.

This Altar Work Notebook will be the place where inspiration is recorded, and miracles are birthed.

This tool can be used to receive inspiration, but it can also be used when you are done carrying a burden.

You can take your pain, your struggles, your grief, fear, self-doubt... you name it and you can place it here.

Hand it over and let God carry it for you.

As you continue to use this tool, you will fine-tune your ability to receive. Just as working out a muscle group each day will strengthen those muscles in time, your "receiving muscle" will strengthen and grow each and every day as you use it. Altar work can help you with any stress or distractions you may have in your life. The creations that you are bringing into this world will come through more quickly, easily, and joyfully as you allow God to lead each step of the way.

ACTION STEPS:

- Grab a notebook that you can dedicate to altar work.

- Spend time in your sacred space utilizing this tool as you need.

- Enjoy the ease that comes from being guided and supported by the Divine!

CHAPTER 12

HEALING BURNOUT

Burnout occurs when we create and don't nourish ourselves. When we create at high levels of energy and action, it takes a lot of our energy. If we don't nourish while in the creative flow, we can drop down really quickly into depression or anxiety.

I have noticed that when I do not nourish myself, resistance and darkness have more impact on me. That's why this chapter is of the highest importance. It will keep you in momentum and out of the dark.

This chapter will guide you through the burnout phase and help you come out of it stronger than ever!

Darkness hits when I am in burnout mode. It's as if my walls become thinner and my resistance to darkness weakens. When burnout hits, we are depleted, exhausted, and more easily susceptible to the darkness.

I want you to take a look back on the last few times you felt like darkness hit. Maybe you call it depression, anxiety, feeling paralyzed . . . or maybe you have just felt like you wanted to stop or quit everything. Maybe you even felt as though darkness was literally encircling you.

However, you experienced it, I want you to think about the days leading up to the darkness you experienced. Were you in burnout mode? Had you recently created something that was way beyond your comfort zone? Did you just launch a new project or were you preparing to launch? Were you vulnerable in your sharing on social media or in inviting someone to sign on with you in a coaching program?

Look at the events that surrounded the days leading up to your breakdown. I am sure you can pinpoint one of these situations above or something similar that broke down your protective layer. Your defenses were down, and the darkness found a crack in the door to sneak in.

Depletion acts in the favor of darkness. And yet, even when I know this, I find that I forget it. Then I end up in burnout mode every single time I push beyond my limits. I find myself in the darkness, trying to find the light.

And so, I created this survival kit for you. It is here to help you in those times when depletion and burnout hit, and you want to have the light return more quickly.

The meditation in this chapter is one of the most powerful meditations I have received. Use it often. It will immediately raise your vibrations.

The survival kit is full of the many things I do when darkness hits. You don't have to do them all, but you can, depending on the severity and heaviness you feel. One thing I know down to my core is this—darkness only hits those who have very important work to do in this world.

So, for each one of you, when the darkness hits, I want you to remember it is proof that you are indeed here to make a difference. You are a Vessel of Light, here to spread more light through the world. Anytime burnout starts to show up, jump into this chapter, and pull the light back in.

Remember—darkness cannot exist within the presence of light. So, the more lighe you can expand throughout your body, the more darkness will dissipate.

And you are light.

ACTION STEPS:

- Pay attention to what your body needs.

- Write down the ideas that come to your mind.

- Listen to and honor what you hear.

- Focus on nourishing and loving your body.

- Listen to the healing burnout mediation here: https://keira-poulsen.mykajabi.com/GodIsMyBusinessPlanBONUS Listen to this as often as you can. It is powerful and will always lift your vibrations.

- Go through The Survival Kit Handout. This has every tool I use when I get stuck in darkness.

- Begin with prayer and healing and then move on to whatever feels good. If things are super dark, then go through the whole list. If you are just trying to pull out of burnout before darkness hits, then pick and choose a handful of tools that you feel drawn to.

CHECKLIST TO GET OUT OF THE DARK

FEAR, RESISTANCE, DARKNESS hits right before a HUGE breakthough. The dark hits before the light appears. Below is a check list to support you through the darkness and into the light.

Have I done my healing work today?
Did I create Sacred Space today? Did I ask for support from my angels?
Did I ignore an inspiration I had been given? If yes, what action can I take to bring that inspiration to earth?
Have I moved my body today? Have I spent time with my feet on the earth?
Have I asked God for ONE action that will help me get OUT of the dark?

SURVIVAL KIT
Awaken the Light

Get Into Your Body

Prayer

Call In Support And
Help From
Your Spiritual Team

Love Yourself

Honor Yourself

You Are A Miraculous
And
Brilliant Being

Healing Practice
1-2 Chakras

Journal

"You Are Light"
Meditation

Shielding Practice

Ask God For One Action To
Feel Better
Then Do That Action

You Are Loved

You Are Worthy

Ask For Divine Guidance

Activate Higher Vibrations
By Learning
Read A Book That
Teaches And Inspires You

You Are More Than Enough, Just As You Are

Follow The "Wants"

Ask Yourself What You
Need To Be Nourished

Do Something Fun

Do Fire Work

Reach Out For Support
From A Therapist/Healer

Read The Book "The Magic"
And Commit To
7 Days Of Gratitude Work

Chanting

Dancing

Do Something To Get
Your Adrenaline Up

CHAPTER 13

UNRAVELING THE
TRUTH ABOUT BUSINESS

Entrepreneurship can be messy. It can be the thing that makes you want to stop; everything. There are many lies that are woven through our interpretation of business. Today my goal is to clean up those lies. It is time that we rewrite our experiences and beliefs around business. It is actually our friend. It is the water that moves our ship forward. It is FUN! It is JOY! It is what helps us create the impact in the world we want to create!

The real truth is—entrepreneurship is creation, and creation is a divine act!

Entrepreneurship is divinely guided creation.

Before we dance in this mess and creation, I invite you to create the space of safety to clear out the old beliefs. Create a sacred space to do this deep work. Invite your Angels and Spiritual Team to help you as you work through your beliefs about business. And then you are going to write down ALL of your belief systems about business.

You can write out these questions on a piece of paper, or you can print off the document from the BONUS page:
https://keira-poulsen.mykajabi.com/GodIsMyBusinessPlanBONUS

CLEARING AND CLEANSING

1. How do you feel about business?

2. What are the thoughts and feelings you have when you think about sales, making money with your gifts, success, and failure?

4. How was your relationship with money when you were a kid?

5. How is your relationship with money now?

6. What fears do you have about running a successful business?

7. What are your fears about failing at business?

8. Write out any fears, anger, rage, or doubts around business.

9. What have been your past experiences with business? Were they good or would you associate business as traumatic and hard?

Write it ALL out!

Let's BURN THIS.

Items to gather:

- Your papers with the written answers

- A fire-safe place to burn

- A fire stick or matches

- A white bowl filled with water

Once you have gathered everything you need, ask for your Spiritual Team to be with you as you move forward with the cleansing work.

Begin by burning the papers. As each word on the pages turns into ash, I want you to breathe deeply into this release. Allow the fire to disintegrate these beliefs.

Once all of the pages have completely burned, you will pick up the ashes and rinse your hands with the ashes. Then you will take the water from the white bowl and rinse your hands in the water until they are clean. To finish, you will take the remaining water and pour it over any remaining ashes. Say out loud, "This is now done and complete." Then you will go back into your sacred space and listen to the meditation above.

When you are finished with the meditation, I invite you to write out the New Truths. Write down how you NOW relate to money, sales, and business.

Let this be the beginning of your friendship with your business.

Great things are ahead when you become friends with your business.

ACTION STEPS:

- Follow the steps outlined in the chapter today for the burning exercise.

- Listen to the meditation provided on the BONUS page: https://keira-poulsen.mykajabi.com/GodIsMyBusinessPlanBONUS

- Write your New Truths.

CHAPTER 14

CREATING A SUCCESSFUL
COACHING OR HEALING BUSINESS

If you feel called to be a coach or be a practitioner of healing… I SEE YOU! This is a soul calling, and I invite you to lean in.

I know that there are many beliefs that will tangle you up in NOT moving forward.

Some may sound like:

- I don't have my shit together… How can I be a coach?

- I am not qualified enough.

- I need more certifications.

- I need more expertise.

- I need to build up my social media presence.

- I am not good enough.

- Who would come to ME?

To all of these I say this:

- Your life qualifies you.

- Your purpose makes you certified.

- No one has their shit together. If that was true, then NO ONE would be helping anyone.

- There is 1 person who needs you right now. You don't need 100k followers. You just need 1.

- Someone is praying for help right now, and your life experiences, your viewpoints, your gifts are THE THING that they are seeking for.

LEAN IN!

TWO FEET.

FULL HEART

FULL TRUST.

This called to you, are you going to listen?

Finding the right clients:

There is so much in the world that will tell you what you need to do to "find your ideal client." And while these are all great and wonderful, they aren't going to be the things that help you create a successful coaching or healing business.

There is healing work that needs to be done to actually allow clients to say YES to working with you. There are spiritual tools that will help you bring those clients into your world. And then there are business tools that will help you create a more fluent and aligned business. Are you ready to make a massive difference while creating success in your work? The next few chapters will be a game-changer in all that you do!

These 3 parts will be broken down over the next several chapters:

- Healing

- Spiritual Tools

- Business Tools

Healing is imperative because it cleans up the messes of the past. If you are resisting clients because of past experiences, then they will not come. The spiritual tools will help you in the energetic magnetism of bringing the perfect clients and customers to you. The business tools in this chapter are simple but will make a big difference in your work.

Jump in, my friends! These three chapters will be a powerful shift in your business and your results!

CHAPTER 15

HEALING WORK
TO RECEIVE CLIENTS

Healing is so deeply important in receiving clients. When you want to lay the groundwork for a successful and abundant coaching and healing practice, it is essential that you clean up the mess first. Similar to a kitchen, I am sure you would prefer to cook a big meal in a clean kitchen instead of in a dirty and cluttered kitchen. Before you can really create success, we must first clean up the mess.

For example, if you are feeling like you aren't good enough to be a coach or a healer, then the "we're open" sign will not be energetically lit. And no one will come your way.

Receiving clients is so much more than writing a post, sending out an email, or running a Facebook ad. It is all about how open you are to receiving those clients. Ask yourself, "Am I actually willing to receive them?"

Many times, we say that we want clients or customers to buy our products. We think that we REALLY want this. But, if we were to go deep inside our Heart Chakra and do some healing work, there might be a few walls that are locked tight.

When your walls are up, nothing gets through.

We first must look at your ability to receive.

I want to share with you, Episode #78 of The Awaken Podcast and a YouTube video on how to receive clients. These will support you in the healing work in your heart chakra. You will find them on the BONUS page. https://keira-poulsen.mykajabi.com/GodIsMyBusinessPlanBONUS

The heart works as a highway of receiving. So, if you want to receive clients, but you have your walls up against love, you won't receive either clients or love. When the highway is closed, nothing gets through.

That is why doing healing work in your heart will shift results in your ability to receive clients. It will also expand your ability to receive love, happiness, support, abundance, and joy. We need to open up the highway of receiving for you to truly receive all that God has in mind for you!

Why would we push away clients?

There are many reasons why we struggle receiving clients.

But it usually has to do with not wanting to connect with others, not wanting to be seen, fear of rejection, fear of being loved and so many other walls.

These walls were placed around your heart for protection and we get to be grateful for the part they played in our lives.

But they also keep you stuck in business and in life.

I have received a healing codex that can help you heal the heart chakra and clear out the heart walls that are pushing clients away.

You can listen to the recording of this healing codex below for you to listen to. Grab it on the BONUS page:

https://keira-poulsen.mykajabi.com/GodIsMyBusinessPlanBONUS

But you can also read it below.

Before you begin this sacred healing codex, go to your sacred space and call in your spiritual team. When we do deep healing work, it is best if we have our angels there to hold the space for us in safety and light.

HEALING CODEX FOR RECEIVING:

The reason why it is so hard to receive is because of pain.

Pain has created heart walls to protect you.

But in an effort to protect, it has kept out the nourishment of love and connection.

Which has left most of your heart chakra to be barren land.

Today we are going to release lava onto barren land. Lava destroys all that it touches. But it also replaces that land with the most fertile soil. The land that is bare, has nothing to be destroyed, and can only gain from the fertile soil that will replace the hot lava.

There is a place within your heart that is bare like this land. We are going to funnel the lava energy to the barren places within you.

These places are bare because there have been times in your life that you opened your heart fully and then pain occurred. When the pain showed up, the walls were placed around your heart to keep you safe. These walls may have been placed there to keep yourself from not being seen, touched, loved, held, desired, wanted and valued. At some point in life, one or all of these things were met with pain. So, it was easier to shut down the receiving of love.

But this cut off the growth that was meant to happen. The growth that only comes from these experiences. There is no shame in these walls. They were placed there as a protector of your safety. Instead of shame, we get to have deep love for these walls. But they are no longer needed. It is time to open up that beautiful heart of yours.

You are not alone in this.

This is the path of being human.

Which is why this codex is here. It will support you planting the new seeds of connection, love, being safe to be seen, heard, witnessed, wanted, desired, and valued.

Are you ready to receive this beautiful codex?

To begin, lay down and notice your breath.

Pay attention to the rise and fall of your chest. I want you to see a golden scarf of light being placed around your third eye and the crown of your head. This is to help quiet the mind right now so that you can let go of the noise and really receive.

Now notice and see if you can feel any pain in your heart. The pain is like a huge dagger that the lava is trying to break up. It's not a landmass that is being broken up; it is your pain that is being broken right now. Up until now, the pain had formed together and created a hard shield around your heart and your body. This was your protective layer. The pain kept everything out.

But this new energy that is rising, is breaking up the pain.

Allow it to do so.

Visualize the hot lava melting the pain. The pain cannot exist within the presence of this lava energy.

Imagine that the pain is similar to an iceberg. The tip is pointing out, which gets snagged quite often. When you feel ignored, unseen, undervalued, or disconnected, these feelings snag the tip of your pain.

This is what creates suffering.

Suffering occurs when our pain gets hit up against over and over again throughout the day and our lives.

But the pain is so much larger than the tip that is sticking out. It goes deep within you and encompasses a larger portion of your body.

Here is why:

Pain is connected to traumatic experiences of connection.

Which then leads to connection = pain.

Don't shame yourself for this pain or these reactions. This is the pathology of pain, especially when it is rooted in any form of trauma.

But, instead have compassion for your pain.

Compassion will allow the iceberg to start to crumble.

To do this, envision a huge iceberg of pain within your body.

The iceberg starts at the base of your pelvis, rises up through your stomach, encompasses your whole heart, and the tip is poking out through your throat.

Imagine that you can see it rumbling, crumbling, as the lava around it starts to melt away the remnants and sections that are being broken off.

I know this is hard.

Pain becomes our friend.

Especially when it feels like it is keeping us safe.

When you shut out connection, being loved, being seen, being desired, wanted and valued- something has to take its place. That is what pain did. Pain is what has held the space open.

Similar to when a child has a tooth pulled too early, there has to be a temporary spacer to hold open the space in the gums until the adult tooth is ready to come in.

Pain was your energetic and emotional spacer until now. We can remove it now that you have chosen to allow the richer state of love, connection, being seen and valued to rise within you.

Sit with this image and allow the lava to disintegrate the pain. Feel the pain be swallowed up in the lava.

Be with this image until the pain in your heart has smoothed out.

The iceberg of pain has melted and has left the barren land.

Is now time to re-code the body and be placed within this rich and dense energetic soil.

Here is how we are going to re-code your body to receive love, connection, safety in being seen, desired, wanted, and valued:

Focus on your heart.

Imagine drawing a connector cable between your heart and your brain. Through that connector cable you can communicate with the brain. It is possible that for a large portion of your life, your emotional heart has been in pain. And because of this pain, your emotional heart had been sending messages to the brain that it was in pain. The brain has been trying to keep you safe from that pain.

We now get to reset that code and the message that has been sent to the brain from your emotional heart. We are going to send the message to your brain that you are safe.

We are going to send the message that you are no longer in pain. And that it is now safe for you to receive love and connection. It is safe to be loved, to be seen, to be heard, to be witnessed, to be desired, wanted and valued.

You are now safe.

Notice how safe you feel.

Start to bring your attention to how peaceful your body is right now at this moment.

Feel the safety within and around you.

As you feel this deep rest and safety, you will begin recording your body.

To reset the messages, imagine that each phrase you speak out loud will be moving through that cable from your heart to your brain. Feel these truths moving from the heart space directly to your brain.

Speak out loud:

> I am safe.
>
> I am safe.
>
> I am safe.
>
> I am safe to be loved.
>
> I am now safe in connection.
>
> I am safe when I am desired.
>
> I am safe when I am valued.
>
> I am safe when I am seen.
>
> I am safe when I am heard.
>
> I am safe when I wanted.
>
> I am safe.
>
> I am safe.
>
> I am safe.
>
> Repeat 3 x.

The re-coding occurs because you are using your senses of feeling, seeing, and speaking these new truths.

You may feel amazing at ease.

And you may have felt a new pain show up.

If you don't, I want you to still stay here with me. The completion of this codex will serve you either way.

But, if you do feel pain, it is the pain of not being able to trust yourself with all of the new emotions that you are feeling.

Allow the lava to melt that pain and any other pain that surfaced during this re-coding.

Allow the lava to melt those fears. They are not true.

Look at you show up for yourself right here and now!

You are your biggest supporter.

You CAN be trusted with all of these new emotions.

You were created for this.

You were created for love.

You were created for connection.

Your soul knows how to do this.

Speak these truths out loud for your ears to witness.

I trust myself.

I trust myself.

I trust myself.

I trust myself

I trust myself with receiving love, connection, being seen, desired, wanted and valued.

I trust myself.

I trust myself.

I trust myself.

Take a deep breath in and thank the communication cord that re-laid these new codes from your heart to your brain.

Wrap the communication cord in light.

Take 3 deep breaths in, allowing the new codes to fully take their place within your body.

To complete the coding, imagine love wrapping you from your feet, up your legs, through your hips into your stomach, spine, lungs. Heart, throat, face, back of the head and then crown.

Be wrapped in your own love.

Allow yourself to be swaddled in God's love for you.

This coding is complete.

ACTION STEPS:

As you move out of this codex, drink water, eat some salt and lay on the earth.

This was powerful work, and you will need to ground back into your body.

Dance, sing, chant, drum, do breathing exercises. GET IN YOUR BODY. It will activate your ability to process that work easier.

CHAPTER 16

SPIRITUAL TOOLS
TO RECEIVE CLIENTS

This chapter is divided into three sections to support you with spiritual tools in receiving clients.

- Spiritually Calling in Your Dream Client

- The Prep Work

- Restoring Your Energy

SPIRITUALLY CALLING IN YOUR DREAM CLIENT

The clients you want to serve are just like YOU! When you work with them, you will feel energized, alive, happy, and on track with your purpose. These are the clients you want to call in. If you don't want to work with someone . . . then DON'T. If you choose to work with someone who you don't want to work with, your energy will stagnate, you will become depleted, and it will shut down the energy of receiving more clients.

When you work with clients who are similar to your energy, who have similar passions and desires in the world, you will leave those sessions feeling alive, and you will also serve them better.

Imagine your dream client. Maybe you have met them, maybe you haven't yet . . . but I want you to imagine this client. What is this person like? Are they filled with passion and action? Are they determined, willing to do what it takes to heal, to create, to make a difference?

Name exactly what you want and then place this version of the dream client on the altar. Ask God to call in your angels to find more clients just like this one, under grace, in perfect ways.

Ask that light will pour over these future clients that they will have abundance to pay for your offerings so you can serve them and support them in their lives. Ask your angels to clear the path so that your clients will be led directly to you.

When we are more detailed with our requests from the Divine, we get better results!

Showing the template of your dream client is one of the easiest ways to receive the perfect clients.

This will happen if you rely on your Spiritual Team to bring in your dream clients.

This is your spiritual marketing.

If you are doing ads, social media posts, Pinterest, podcasting, or any other formal marketing tools, you can add a BONUS energy to each form of physical marketing with these spiritual tools. Ask your angels to take your Facebook ad to the exact clients that you want to work with. Ask your angels to take your Instagram post and place them in the feed of the clients who need your work.

This has proven to be a wild success in my work, and I know it will work for you as well!

ACTION STEPS:

- Begin using the Spiritual Tools to call in your dream clients!

- Write out the DREAM client. And then ask for your angels to go and find them!

THE PREP WORK

Coaching and healing are two of the most powerful ways we can show up as a Vessel of Light. Because of this, the prep work we do before we meet with a client is of the highest importance. There must be at least 5–10 minutes before you meet with a client for you to push away your own stress, your own problems, and get into your body. There needs to be a conscious effort to do a practice like The Sacred Creative Process, and truly surrender this session to God.

Being a healer or coach doesn't mean you have your life figured out.

NO ONE does.

Instead, it means you are dedicated to being a vessel for those you are coaching. You are agreeing to show up, be a vessel to bring the work down that they are needing, and then teach them how to do that on their own.

It is my deepest belief that we are not here to coach or heal people for a period of years. Instead, we are here to kickstart their light. We are facilitating their growth so that they can become the leaders they are here to become.

Everyone was created to lead, to make a difference, and to use their gifts. As coaches, we are here to remind our clients of that truth. We get to teach them about the tools that have served us and helped us expand into our gifts.

There will be days when you are scheduled to coach, but your world is tipping. This is normal for creators. When we choose to do big things, walls crash down. And you might have that happen right before a coaching call. If you can ask God to take your burdens and the brokenness that you feel while inviting the Divine to run that coaching call, you will see miracles happen. That session will be a miracle because you will become 100% clear that YOU did not coach, but that the Divine worked THROUGH you.

Having a prep practice before you coach or heal will change the dynamics of your business. This is what will make your session powerful and life changing!

ACTION STEPS:

- Put your prep practice into use each time you meet with a client this week.

- And if you don't have clients, use the following method after you have spent time with another individual.

RESTORING YOUR ENERGY AFTER YOUR SESSIONS

After you coach or facilitate healing work with a client, there is a very important process that needs to happen. This is the "clean-up" work and the restoration of your energy and being.

No matter how shielded you are, it is nearly impossible to NOT take on any of your client's energy.

Imagine if you were walking around with bits and pieces from every client you work with. Can you see how heavy your energy would become? This aspect of having a successful coaching or healing business is so important and is vital to the success of your work.

I like FAST and IMMEDIATE results. For the fastest clean out of your energetic system is sound healing.

I use my drum and drum over my heart, and around my body to clear out the energy I picked up.

I also use my sound bowl and I place it directly onto my heart. I play the sound bowl and hum to allow the sound to clear out my system, FAST and QUICK.

But, if you don't have sound tools, below is a powerful practice that works with potency.

This practice takes about 3–10 minutes.

The Clean-Up:

- If you can lie down somewhere, that would be best, but sitting will also work if that is your only option.

- Set the timer on your phone for 3–10 minutes, depending on the time you have. Setting the timer on your phone will allow you to fully relax and do the work that is needed without minding the time.

- Turn on meditation music of your choice. (I love Wayne Dyer's "I Am That I Am.")

- If you can, place a selenite crystal on your heart, solar plexus, or naval.

- Close your eyes and take a few deep breaths in. Really focus on breathing all the way down into your lower belly.

- Imagine the Divine Light pouring over your body. If you are lying flat, imagine the light encompassing your whole body at once, like a heatwave or a full circle of light around you. If you are sitting, imagine the light coming in through the Crown Chakra and moving down through every part of your body.

- Visualize this light wrapping each cell in your body. As the light wraps each cell, ask the light to cleanse anything and everything that isn't yours and disintegrate it so that it will be completely gone. Ask that the light cleanse everything that you picked up from that session with your client. Sit with this for a few minutes to allow a deep and thorough clean-up.

The Restoring:

- After you have visualized and done the clean-up, imagine that the light is now going within each and every cell of your body and igniting the light within the nucleus of each cell.

- Watch the Divine Light begin to dance and ebb throughout your body! Really allow yourself to receive the restoration of your energy, your health, your joy, and your vitality!

- Finish with shielding and take a final deep breath into your Sacral Chakra.

If you implement this simple yet profound practice after every client, you will find that you have more energy, more passion, and more to give.

ACTION STEPS:

- Find a method to use after you work with a client.

- CLEAN and CLEAR YOU, and you will have so much more to give!!

CHAPTER 17

SELFLESS SELLING

SALES CALLS.

These two words can stop an entrepreneur in their tracks. It can feel slimy, gross, scary and conjure so many other lower vibrational feelings.

Why?

Because so many of us have been on the other side of a slimy sales call. We have had those awkward messages slide into our DM's where we just feel like an object to be sold to. And for this reason, we don't want to be in sales!

This has always been my experience with sales. I hated them. I refused to do sales . . . until one day I was the recipient of an extraordinary sales call.

I was calling to inquire about joining Richie Norton's mastermind. I knew I was getting on a sales call to learn more about his mastermind.

And this "sales call" changed my life.

Richie hired Ben Willson to take his sales calls.

Ben was looking for ways to increase his marketing and sales influence.

Richie taught Ben his unique sales call strategy and asked him to take his inbound calls. And Ben changed my business in a one-hour phone call.

Everything changed when I experienced this sales call.

This call wasn't about the mastermind. It wasn't about what I was getting or how much it would cost. No, this "sales call" had nothing to do with the mastermind.

Instead, Ben wanted to know about me. He asked me questions that no one has ever asked me. He wanted to know WHO I was and what my dreams were. He listened and he cared.

And because of that, I joined the mastermind.

Richie's mastermind changed how I create business and interweave it with mothering 5 kids. He taught me his brilliant concept of "Anti-Time Management." My income tripled in 2 months. My time spent with my kids expanded. And my whole business model changed! Richie changed my life.

I needed to join his mastermind.

But if the sales call had sucked, I would have NEVER joined.

Instead, Ben saw me, witnessed my greatness, and LISTENED to me. And so I said yes, and my life changed.

I didn't realize what had occurred until Ben and Richie did a podcast talking about this type of sales call. And I was the client Ben referred to on the podcast. Receiving and then listening to the method Richie had taught Ben transformed my whole experience with sales.

The basis of what I am teaching you in this chapter are what Richie Norton taught and Ben Willson. And then Ben shared them with me. You can listen to Richie and Ben's podcast here: https://richie.libsyn.com/coaching-how-to-do-a-proper-sales-call-without-selling

I then added my spiritual tools to the amazing sales model they taught me.

What I want YOU to get out of this chapter is simply this:

THE SALES CALL IS EQUAL IN IMPORTANCE TO WHAT YOU OFFER.

You can have the most extraordinary program that changes lives 100% of the time, but if you don't know how to bring people into your program—NO ONE'S life changes.

The sales call is the bridge of safety that brings clients into your amazing program.

Let me put that into a different form so you really get this.

When we suck at sales (for any reason at all) people's lives DON'T change.

When you don't create safety for them, when you talk OVER them, when you don't listen—they don't join your program or purchase your offering. And remember: your program IS going to change their lives. Your offering is exactly what they need.

So, you need to be able to sell.

But not in the gross way.

Sell in the most powerful and successful way.

Selfless Selling is what I call this form of sales.

The main focus of *Selfless Sales* is to listen to, witness the greatness of, and then create the space for the beautiful human you are talking to be heard and have a life-changing experience.

You want to them to feel heard, seen, and loved on this call.

Their life changes in one sales call with you.

And then when they do say **yes**, their results will be me 100x more powerful!

This form of selling is so impactful because these sales calls are healing sessions.

Why?

Because when someone is HEARD—*they heal.*

I am going to say that again: When YOU HEAR THEM—**THEY HEAL.**

How often are people asked about their dreams, their purpose, their vision . . . and actually HEARD?

When does someone get to share into a space of belief and safety? It is your honor to hold that space for them. And when you do, they will heal. And that call will change their lives.

If they are the right fit—they WILL join you or purchase your offering.

I say, "right fit," because YOU are an important aspect to this equation.

You want to be a **HOLY HELL YES** to bringing them into your programs.

Not everyone is the perfect fit for YOU, which means that when you are on the sales call with them, listening to and hearing them, you get to listen to **you** as well.

What does your heart say?

I call this the **Holy Hell Yes** test.

If your heart is OPEN and saying "YESSS" to what they are sharing, and you know that you can serve them—then it is a perfect match! Offer the program, the mastermind, your coaching, your product, and serve them! Offer what you know is going to support them AND you.

It is easy to invite everyone to join or buy your offerings. We are taught "more is better."

But it is imperative to your success and the success of your client that you are a **HOLY HELL YES,** first.

If you feel:

- A weird feeling about bringing them in
- Uneasy
- That you will need to "pull" them along
- Or any other sensation that doesn't feel "right"

I would invite you to pray about it; ask for guidance and direction before you invite them in.

You have the right to choose who works with you.

One of my favorite coaches and friends, Dr. Benjamin Hardy, calls this concept, **"Always be the Buyer."**

Which means even when you are selling, you are also buying. You are choosing who joins your energetic world.

Selfless Sales is healing for both sides.

You listen to and hear their needs, *which heals them.* You also listen to YOU and your needs, *which heals you.*

When you follow this formula, your sales will increase, your energy will be activated, and everyone will get the best results possible!

So... are you ready to step into this beautiful way of selling?

Let's do this.

Let's clear out the OLD ways, and start selling from the heart, from love, and from service.

SALES CALL PREP:

The sales call starts before you even get on the call with your potential client. It begins with your heart in the space of service.

Before each sales call, I prepare with my prayer below and then move into **The Sacred Creative Process.**

> *You can use the prayer below until you create the words that fit best with your soul and with your own words. This is just a template to support you in this practice.*

SELFLESS SALES PREP PRAYER:

"God, please help me to surrender my needs and my wants.

Help me to be selfless and in deep, true service.

God, help me to see his/her needs.

Help me to hear his/her needs.

Help me to know if I can help him/her expand in his/her gifts, in his/her abilities, and towards his/her full purpose.

Show me how to help him/her say YES to himself/herself!

Clear out any resistance that I might have that would prevent him/her from saying yes.

Clear out any of his/her resistance that wants to keep him/her playing small and hidden.

Help me to hear my needs and my intuition.

Let me know if I can serve him/her to the best of my abilities to serve him/her and activate my own energy.

God, lead this call so that it may be in the highest good for all."

Sales CONVERSATION:

ASK and then LISTEN.

The questions will come to you. But the truth is: you won't be talking.

You will be listening.

You will hear them, and then hear them, and then hear them.

But here are a few questions to get you started:

1. **Start with asking them about their life.**

2. **Ask them why they scheduled this call with you.**

3. **Ask what their vision is for their (insert what you help people with).**

For example: Ask what their vision is for their business, their healing, their dreams, their creations, their book, their family, their relationship, etc.

4. **Ask what they have been struggling with.**

5. **Ask what support would make the difference for them.**

Once you have heard their dreams, their visions, and their struggles, you get to determine two things:

1. Can you help them? Do you have a program, product, or coaching practice that can help them solve their problem?

2. Are you a HOLY HELL YES to serve them?

If you can answer yes to both of these questions, THEN you can offer up that **you have a solution for them.**

Articulate their problem (as you understand it) clearly for them and share that your (offering) solves that problem.

Share with them that you want to support them in getting to the SOLUTION.

This is where you can share what you are offering.

Share minimally. Bullet point what you share.

The truth is hard. But here it is:

NO ONE cares about your program, your offerings, or your products.

I know that is rough to hear, but it's true.

No one actually cares.

If you share for 15 minutes about everything that you created and how awesome it is and how it will change their lives—*you just lost them.*

All of the healing that occurred when you listened to them got deleted with your oversharing about YOU.

Your program is YOU.

That's not what this call is about. This call is about THEM.

So, share what is necessary. The basics. And then share with them the results they will get.

Simple and clean is all that is needed.

Then share the price and sit.

Don't get wobbly. If you wobble, they wobble.

TWO FEET THIS.

You charge what you charge because you CHOSE that price.

You chose it, so don't wobble.

Stand firm in WHO you ARE.

Those who see you and know that you have the solution they are looking for will figure out a way to make it happen.

P.S. those are my favorite clients: the ones who don't have the money but find a way to figure it out. Why? Because they are hungry! Hungry for results which means they will get results.

So, name the price and two feet the hell out of that moment.

YOU ARE IT.

You ARE the path to helping them get their solutions.

HOLY HELL YES, this moment with a full heart and they will say yes!

Summary on Selfless Sales:

A nice reminder of what doesn't work in a successful selfless sales call:

- Rush for them to stop talking so you can tell them ALL about your amazing program.

- Spend most of the time talking about how you can help them.

- Talk about yourself, your journey, and why you do what you do.

- Talk about the results you are going to give them.

- Go in detail of EVERYTHING they will get if they work with you.

- Let them think about it without a definite timeline of when they can join.

- Over talk, over share, take up most of the call talking.

- Focus on selling them only one program or product.

- Selfish selling is when you have an agenda in mind, and you want to get someone to join you there. (Like getting onto a call and focusing on how to sell them into a certain program or product).

Here is what DOES work:

- Listen

- Listen

- Listen

- Ask them more questions.

- Ask more about their goals and dreams.

- Ask them what they need.

- Ask them what they want.

- Listen

- Listen

- Listen

- If you have the solution to their needs—**OFFER THAT.**

- Sell them whatever program, product, or offer will fit THEIR need.

- Selfless selling is when you offer them the solution to whatever their problem is.

- If you don't have the solution to their needs—**don't sell them anything.** Honor them. And let them know that you don't offer the service that they need. But do you know someone who does? Can you refer them out?

- After you offer, *then* ask them if that feels like what they are looking for.

- If they say yes, then **ask them to join** you in this program.

- You can offer a special 24-hour bonus discount or a 24-hour BONUS if they pay up front. Whatever will serve them best and help them join sooner than later—you create magic for them. You want to help them join quickly, because the fear and doubt brain will show up for them, holding them hostage to their old self. You are here to liberate them and support them into saying yes to themselves!!

  o **If they say yes:**

    ▪ When they say yes, CELEBRATE with them!

- Look right into their eyes and congratulate them. Congratulate them on making this amazing decision! And then speak truths. What AMAZINGNESS do you see in them? Share your heart. Tell them what is present for you! You see their greatness. Share with them what you see!

- Send an email right after the call and welcome them in! Plus, send them the contract and links for them to use for payment.

  o **If they say that they need to think about it or talk to a spouse**:

    - Let them know that you can send them a link and that you will hold this special discount or bonus for 24 hours. They can join whenever they want, but the discount or bonus ends in 24 hours.

    - Then pause.

    - Let them answer.

    - Bite your tongue if you need to! DON'T make this about you.

- After the call, before the 24-hour marker:

  o Send out an email; keep it short and let them know that the 24-hour marker is almost there and invite them to jump into your program to get the result that they want. Then put in the link for the contract and payment again.

  o **If they don't click, reach out. DM them, email them, or text them. Follow up with them. Help them remember their dreams. This is where you are a warrior for them! Fight for their dream!**

YOU ARE a HUGE piece to them achieving that dream.

Fight for them.

But . . . if they don't respond, then wrap them in love and let them go. Pray for them that the right coach/program will show up for them. Release their energy and open up for those who are a **Holy Hell Yes to work with you!**

This is it.

The whole purpose of *Selfless Sales* is to SERVE.

These are NOT sales calls.

These are YOU helping them say yes to themselves.

These calls are you inviting them to say YES to their souls.

These calls are you offering the programs and products THEY NEED.

Regular Sales Calls are:

❖ Trying to get people to buy your program or product

❖ Having an agenda already set in your mind and not hearing what they need

❖ Convincing people that what you have to offer is good enough for them to buy

❖ Saying what you think they want to hear

❖ Focusing on YOUR needs and wants

***Selfless Sales* Calls are:**

❖ You are filling the need of the customer

❖ You are providing them with the service that will solve the problem that they have

❖ You are giving them the puzzle piece they have been searching for

❖ You are giving them the tools that will help them expand into their greatness and worth

❖ Listening, listening, listening to what they need, what their dreams are, and what results they want

For most of your customers, you will be listening in a way they haven't been listened to in a while. Maybe you are listening to them in a way that they have *never* experienced.

This is healing work.

Remember: this is a healing session, not a sales call.

Selfless Sales reaffirms that their dreams are important, that they are worth investing in themselves, and that *everything is possible.*

You want them to leave a sales call having felt seen in their greatness, seen in their gifts, and HEARD for the brilliant being that they truly are.

This is more than sales.

This is more than money.

This is how you impact humanity—one person at a time.

CHAPTER 18

HOW TO CHANNEL
YOUR BOOK

Writing a book that is directed by God is a sacred experience. Allowing yourself to get out of the way and instead allow for light to move through you into your hands and onto the pages of a book *is sacred*. There is a deep reverence that I hold for channeling your writing. There are 2 different practices that I believe help us write spiritually.

FIRST PRACTICE: CHANNEL WRITING

This is going to be the process we use over and over to create, guided by the Divine.

- Create a sacred space that is dedicated to receiving.

- Do the Sacred Creative Process that you learned in chapter 7.

- Begin to write.

Allow the light to move through your hands and watch as words come through you that you didn't expect, know, or plan.

Witness the beauty of God working through you.

SECOND PRACTICE: THE RECEIVING BOWL

- Imagine that you have a spiritual bowl over your heart. It is always there, open to receive.

- Put your prayer up to God each day, asking that the content of your book will come down into your mind, heart, and hands.

- Then go about your day in faith, knowing that it will come through.

- Have a separate notebook dedicated to your new book you are writing and each time you receive ideas, put them down into this notebook. Or you can use the notes app or the voice memos on your phone to record the ideas that come to you.

- Then ask God and your angels to open up time and space for you to sit with all of the notes and insights you have received.

- After doing The Sacred Creative Process, sit with all that you have received and allow God to guide you in the order of the notes you have been receiving.

I use both of these practices when I write my books.

I set aside dedicated time to receive, but then I always ask for inspiration to be dropped in.

Play with both and see what feels best for you.

And if you want to get a kickstart to your channeling journey, book a spot on my morning show. I will spend 30 minutes with you, channeling your book through! Grab a spot on my calendar here:

https://keira-poulsen.mykajabi.com/GodIsMyBusinessPlanBONUS

PRAYER OF LIGHT

PREP TO RECEIVE

I ask that Light will touch my ears that I may hear what needs to be heard.

I ask that Light will touch my third eye that I will have access to all of my spiritual gifts.

I ask that Light will touch my lips that I speak only what needs to be spoken.

I ask that Light will touch my arms down to my fingertips, that I write only what needs to be written.

CHAPTER 19

CLEAR THE PATH
TO BECOMING AN AUTHOR

To become an author means we are willing to look at our STUFF. And that brings up major STUFF.

But really, I hear these questions from so many people who want to become authors.

They say:

- Who am I to write a book?

- What if no one reads it?

- What if it's not good?

- There are too many people talking about this topic, why would I write about this?

These thoughts are just roadblocks. They are blocking the road that you are meant to travel. The road to changing peoples' lives!!

They are lies and illusions.

Lies and illusions that keep you small, stuck, and sadly, leaving the world WITHOUT the message that is burning in your soul.

You see, these lies are fed from the ego, resistance, and darkness, hoping to keep you small and to hide the light that is asking to come through you.

But SERVICE trumps ALL of those things.

Service deletes lies.

I have an amazing video for you on this topic. Grab it on the BONUS page here: https://keira-poulsen.mykajabi.com/GodIsMyBusinessPlanBONUS

But since you are HERE…. let's go through some journal prompts to support you in waking up the SERVICE.

- Who NEEDS your book?

_____

_____

_____

_____

_____

_____

- What does their life look like right now? What are they struggling with? What are they praying for right now?

_____

_____

_____

_____

_____

_____

- What would their life look like IF they read your book? What results
  want them to have?

  _____

  _____

  _____

  _____

  _____

  _____

- How would you feel if you didn't write this book?

  _____

  _____

  _____

  _____

  _____

  _____

I am here to tell you that someone needs your book.

They need YOUR message.

It is vital that you bring it through.

For them. But also, for YOU.

When you hold a book inside of you, it begins to take your energy. You become tired, overwhelmed and distracted.

The book is full of energy. It can give you energy or it can weigh you down.

But when you birth it and bring it to the world, **it GIVES YOU LIFE!**

This book will wrap you in a river of momentum.

And here is why… When you channel a book, you are in the vibrational frequency of God.

When you are in that Divine frequency- *EVERYTHING works better.*

Actually, miracles abound in that energy.

So… it is imperative that you write this book.

FOR YOU AND THE WORLD.

Bring it through and receive the magic that is waiting for you.

CHAPTER 20

THE BUSINESS
OF BEING AN AUTHOR

Many believe it is hard to become a published author. But the truth is . . . it is simple when you know the steps.

There are many publishing houses, but I would love to invite you to apply to be a Freedom House author!

Apply here: https://keira-poulsen.mykajabi.com/GodIsMyBusinessPlanBONUS

I created Freedom House Publishing Co. to be a House of Freedom.

It is a house of liberation.

We liberate authors as they share their messages to the world and then we liberate readers as they are impacted by the written word.

Freedom House only publishes books that inspire, teach, and heal.

I believe that there is power in bringing together authors who are divinely guided in one publishing house.

We publish HUGE authors, and we publish authors who have 1 follower on social media.

That's why we are so different.

We don't choose our authors based off of the following they have, or the size of their email list.

We choose them based on their heart.

Do you want to change the world with your message?

Do you have a BURNING message waiting to explode goodness into the world?

Do you want to be a part of a powerful community of leaders who have the same desires to change humanity for the better?

These are our requirements.

We seek those who want to impact the world with more light.

That may be in the entrepreneurial space.

It may be in parenting.

Or maybe healing, spirituality, or Divine guidance.

The topic doesn't matter.

The heart does.

The logo of Freedom House is the sun.

Because the sun cleans and creates.

It clears and heals.

The books that we publish clears out old beliefs and old ways that no longer work.

They create NEW.

New pathways, new beliefs and NEW results!

If you are ready to bring this message out of your heart, and onto paper- then I invite you to lean in and receive.

Receive the book and then publish it.

It didn't come to you to sit in a word doc on your computer! **It came to you to SERVE.**

Let your book be seen, heard and witnessed.

Allow it to do the work it was always created to do.

CHAPTER 21

BLESSING YOUR BOOK

I believe that when you publish your book and you hold it in your hands, a ceremony and a blessing of light can make a profound difference.

Intention IS everything.

This ceremony will code your book with your intentions. We want people to be able to pick up your book and immediately feel a shift in their body.

That is what this ceremony will do.

CEREMONY OF BLESSING YOUR BOOK:

- Find a sacred space to sit with your book

- Hold the book in your hands and move through this visualization:

  o Ask that the Divine Light will be poured through your book. Ask that the Divine Light wrap every letter on each page of your book with love so that every reader who reads these words will be encircled in love. Ask that the words on the page transform each reader's life. This book is here to activate them, to raise their vibrations, and to transform them. You can also add any other blessings upon your book and those who read it as you do this ceremony.

Remember, this book came to you with light. You now get to do the energetic work to activate the light within the book. I believe that this is how we help transform the world energetically.

ACTION STEPS:

You can do this ceremony with your book before you hit publish or right when you get the first published book!

Bless it and then send it out to the world!

CHAPTER 22

HOW TO CREATE AND LAUNCH A PODCAST

PODCASTING.

It is one of the most spiritual and sacred things I have been blessed to be a part of. Podcasting is a sacred space. You get to hold this space in deep love and reverence for being a Vessel of Light. Your words will come through into someone's ear and change their day, their week, or even their life.

The vibration of your voice can actually change the vibration within the person who is listening. This is something I do not take lightly. Writing a podcast, guided by God, is a powerful role to take. This is why I take so much care in the spiritual prep leading up to an episode.

If it is a solo episode:

- I begin my prep by sending up a prayer, asking God to show me what topic the episode should cover.

- I then keep my heart open for a few days and take note of any ideas, insights, or impressions that come to me.

- Then I ask my Spiritual Team to hold open a place and time for me to write the episode.

- I usually use my sacred space time in the early mornings to receive. I use The Sacred Creative Process and then begin to write.

- This process has been one that surprises me time and time again. I watch as a whole podcast will come out of my hands that had never even been in my mind, or I see an expansion of the ideas that had been coming to me. It is a beautiful experience.

- As I have been podcasting for 3 years now, I actually don't pre-write my episodes. I just sit down and ask God to speak through me. This has been a powerful experience of co-creating with God.

If you have a guest on the show:

- Before they get on the show, ask your angels to pour some light over them, allowing their day to be clear and easy, and prepping them for the show.

- Call in both of your angels before the show to participate and help with the message.

- Do The Sacred Creative Process with them before the episode.

Before either episode, you can ask that light will be poured through the internet connection and that it will be clean and clear for the whole episode. You can also ask that light will be room, your voice, and the vibrations moving through the episode.

These simple practices will help you show up as your Divine Self for your episodes. These practices will make everything easier. They will help you create a sacred and powerful experience for you, your guests, and your listeners!

They will also clear out any "ums, likes" dead spaces and mess ups.

Where to host your podcast:

There are many different host sites to host your podcast from. I have used Libsyn from the beginning and have loved it.

ACTION STEP:

- Set up an account on https://libsyn.com.

- Begin to ask God to start pouring your podcast episodes into your heart.

Step-by-Step Guide on Setting Up Your Podcast

1. Ask God to help you see a vision for this podcast.

2. Ask God to help you hear/see what the name of this podcast should be.

3. Begin making an image that you will use as your podcast image. Start looking at other podcasts and see if you can get some ideas. I personally believe it is better with your picture on it. That way, people can connect to you better as they listen. If you can, get a professional headshot done for your image.

4. Buy your equipment. I recommend the Blue Yeti with a pop filter. You can find it on Amazon.

5. Make your sound booth. Grab a trifold from Walmart or your nearest store and order sticker foam from Amazon. You will place the sticker foam to the inside of your trifold. Put together this mini sound booth for under $20! When you have created it, place it around your mic to help support you sound better.

6. Create your intro. This is going to be about 15–30 seconds of you introducing your podcast and giving the intention of your podcast. (Take a minute to listen to one of my episodes at the beginning. The first 30 seconds of my episode is the intro: The Sacred Writing Podcast. Your intro will play at the beginning of each one of your shows. As always, I encourage you to ask God what the intro should be. What do you want your listeners to know about your show? What can they expect from listening to your podcast? Pick the music that will play in your intro. Pick a song from a royalty-free website. I like www.indiemusicbox.com, but there are many websites to get royalty-free music for about $5–$15: Purchase and download your music.

7. Editing. You have 2 choices here. You can learn how to edit your own podcast. But, if you are ok spending $35–$80 per week on podcast editing and audiograms, then I would encourage you to look at Fiverr. Fiverr is a great source of podcast editing. If you are working with an editor, you will send the zoom audio file (not the video) and the music to the editor. Then ask them to put those together with your podcast intro.

8. Record your first 3 episodes. You want to follow all of the spiritual tools you have learned as you record this: The Sacred Creative Process.

9. Ask that the Divine Light will pour through the internet to keep it clean, stable, and strong during your recording. You can ask God to pour down the episode in writing first (if you are doing a solo episode) or you can show up to the mic and ask God to work through you, right there in the moment. If you have a guest on the show, remember the spiritual tools of pouring light over them before they jump on the call. I encourage you to do some sort of "praying it in" with your guest to center, ground, and prepare for the sacred work that is about to happen.

   1. Episode 1: It is my belief that episode 1 should be you alone. In this episode, you are laying the groundwork for this whole podcast. Introduce who you are. Talk about your desires and intentions for this podcast. What path have you walked that has brought you here? This episode is how your guests will get to know you, why you are doing this, and what you plan for your podcast going forward. Imagine this as an introduction to a new friend, but not just any friend—a new soul friend.

2. Send your 3 episodes to your editor (or edit them yourself).

3. Set up your Libsyn account.

4. Ask your editor if they can get your podcast up on ALL the podcast platforms. This should take 10 days from the time they begin their work. I know it costs about $200 with my editor, but I'm not sure what the cost is with other editors.

5. Upload your podcast to Libsyn.

6. SHARE, SHARE, SHARE! Starting 2 weeks before your podcast will be live, I want you to begin promoting, dropping hints, and sharing what is coming out with your Instagram following, Facebook, and email list. People like to get excited. If you can drip this launch, there will be many who celebrate with you when it goes live!!

7. Start asking God to bring you episode ideas weekly. Ask God to start showing you the guests for your show and watch the miracles flow in.

8. Pick a day and time that you are releasing your podcast every week and enjoy this beautiful and amazing experience of podcasting.

ACTION STEPS:

Follow the guide above and BEGIN!

CHAPTER 23

HOW TO CREATE AND LAUNCH
A DIGITAL COURSE

Creating a digital course is one of the TOP ways to serve hundreds, thousands, and hundreds of thousands of people at a time. It is the fastest way to teach powerful principles to MANY people, ALL OVER the world! And it can seem daunting. But, like everything you learn here in "God is My Business Plan,", it can be easy when you create *guided by the Divine*.

Creating a digital course is HARD when you rely on your own wisdom, knowledge, and other people's opinions. Doing this is a sure way to never complete it. But if you choose to go to God and ask for guidance, it will always flow through you with ease.

STEPS TO CREATING A SUCCESSFUL COURSE:

- Ask God to show you the name or concept of the course you are here to create.

- Begin to open up your heart and mind to receive ideas, concepts, and classes for the course.

- Let them show up like flowers. They don't need to come in a perfect line. Let them blossom in all the different ways and times.

- Once you have received some great ideas and have taken notes on them, sit down in a space dedicated to creating with God.

- Follow the Sacred Creative Process.

- Begin to ask God to show you the first class. Use the notes, the insights, and inspirations given to you and watch your course unfold before your eyes!

- Remember, God's time is NOT our time.

Sometimes we create exactly what God inspired us to create but don't see immediate success. Don't worry. There is always a plan in place. Sometimes God inspires us to write a course that will one day be a part of a HUGE course that ends up being extremely successful. But if you hadn't written the other one a year earlier, the course wouldn't be complete.

Don't doubt what you are given. Trust the inspiration. Trust the divine timing. Trust that you are in the creation of divine messages coming through you. Follow this practice time and time again as you write courses.

There are many courses inside of you. Don't stop creating. Each course builds on the others. Each course will lead people to where they need to go. And you will watch the wisdom of God unfold in your life as you create these courses, one step at a time.

ACTION STEPS:

If you have had a digital course inside of you that you know wants to come through, then your homework is to BEGIN!

Start the process by following all of the steps in this book.

If you have never had the idea to create a digital course, then your homework is to ask for inspiration from the Divine and see if this is something that would serve humanity and your business!

How to Technically Build Your Digital Course

For many people, writing a course is the easy part, but getting it onto a digital platform is where they get stuck. But rest assured, once you learn HOW to do it, you will be able to create digital courses all day long!

The truth is, when you learn how to create a digital course, you can always create MORE! As you learn more tools and expand in your work, you can create more and more courses to serve your clients!

I use Kajabi.

I love it!! I have used many other platforms, but Kajabi holds everything you need, from landing pages to email sequences to digital courses. That's why we are going to use this format in this book.

If you would like to sign up for Kajabi below is my personal link that you can use:

https://app.kajabi.com/r/vswXJ95o

I have created many videos for my clients on how to use Kajabi. But the truth is- Kajabi has the BEST "how to" videos.

Google what you need, and you will find it in an amazing Kajabi video!

CHAPTER 24

HOW TO MAKE
A POWERFUL VIDEO

Making a powerful video shift EVERYTHING! Not only is this very important in your digital courses, but it is essential in your marketing material. Stats show that video is what converts. I believe it is because when someone sees you in video, they FEEL your energy, and that creates trust with you. Making a powerful video is going to be one of your best tools.

STEPS:

1. Get a tripod with a light. I get mine on Amazon for $30 or less.

2. Have light coming in ON your face from a window, if possible.

3. Look at the camera hole when you talk, NOT at your face. When you look at your face, it automatically disconnects you from your audience. When you look into the camera, it connects you directly to your audience. It makes them feel as though you are speaking to them.

4. Ground yourself before you speak. Take 3 deep breaths.

5. Do The Sacred Creative Process before you shoot the video.

6. EDIT. I believe more light creates better energy! I always edit my videos with VSCO, which is an app on your phone.

ACTION STEPS:

Make 1 video a day for a week using these tools. Get comfortable in front of the camera. And then begin creating marketing videos for Instagram, YouTube, and of course, your digital courses.

CHAPTER 25

TECH MADE EASY

TECHNOLOGY.

I know—many hate it. It can be the one thing that stands between you and your success. So, I am here to make it easy. If you have a program that is dialed in with the right tech software, your life will change, and your business will change simply by knowing what tools to use.

I believe that we also can have some serious problems with technology because we don't want to learn it, and I get that. But I am also telling you that when you choose to embrace tech, your business will begin to THRIVE, and you will feel so supported.

That is what technology is. It is a support system that will work for you while you play, create, parent, work, and have fun! So, let's rewire your thoughts about tech and begin accepting the support that is available to you.

MY FAVORITE TECH TOOLS:

- Kajabi for creating digital courses, landing pages, opt-in pages, email sequences, and membership sites: https://app.kajabi.com/r/vswXJ95o

- Acuity for booking clients, podcasts, sessions, etc.: https://acuityscheduling.com

- VSCO for video and photo editing

- iMovie for cutting the videos that you make for your digital courses

ACTION STEPS:

- Begin playing around with the tech above.

- Experiment with tech.

CHAPTER 26

SOCIAL MEDIA
DONE SPIRITUALLY

INSTAGRAM.

You either hate it or love it. Today, I want to help you reframe whatever experience you have had with Instagram.

It is my belief that Instagram is our modern-day "wall." In ancient times, the messengers, thought leaders, and prophets would stand on walls to share the messages they had been inspired to share. Those messages weren't always received, and sometimes they were. Something that stands out to me about those people is the willingness they had to give the message, *no matter what.*

I know that social media is tainted with false perfection, jealousy, competition, and can really warp and mess with our self-esteems. But what if you could imagine it being your "wall?"

What if everything you created and shared via Instagram and Facebook was only what you felt guided to share? Would that change how you feel about sharing? Would this change how you feel about how many "likes" or "comments" you got on a post?

I believe it could.

A message that is guided by the Divine has nothing to do with you. Those likes and comments have nothing to do with your worth. You are the messenger. You are here to bring light and new truth to help humanity.

My invitation to you is this: with every post you make this week, let it be guided. Share the post and pour light through it so that it may find those who need it, and then walk away. Don't look at the likes. I mean it—**don't look.** If someone comments, respond and walk away.

This is only your wall. Let it be the wall and allow yourself to be the vessel. Be the window of light for someone scrolling through a thread of competitive, perfection-tainted posts. Let your post stop them in their tracks as they feel the light coming through every word you were guided to write. Allow light to be the stream that carries your work into the world!

ACTION STEPS:

For the next 5 days, let every post you make be guided. If you don't post often, I invite you to post 1–2 times this week using this method!

CHAPTER 27

LANDING PAGES
AND EMAIL SEQUENCES

Understanding how to create landing pages and email sequences is essential in your work. Without this tech, you will be showing up to events with a piece of paper, asking people to write their email address down (which is totally fine, but it limits you to only events.)

What if every person who showed up at your Instagram or Facebook page could get something from you and you could get their email? Can you see how much more efficient that would be?

Having their email brings them into your world. They get to join your work because now they can get special messages from you via email. They get to know about all of your programs, books, and products. If you don't have a landing page, then you are keeping people out of your world. The landing page brings them in. The email sequence is the best thing that has ever been invented!

Imagine creating a 5-part email series. One that lights you up. One that is guided by God, and the messages are amazing. Now, imagine that you have to send out each email separately, 5 times, to everyone you want to send it to. Ugh! But, with an automated email sequence, you write it ONE TIME, and people can be getting those emails ALL day because they will be automatically sent after that person goes to your landing page.

So, you could be playing with your kids, eating out, or working with clients, and emails are being sent out. It's genius and it will change your business. I encourage you to try it.

Spend time researching Kajabi email sequence and landing pages.

Also… my FAV hack is to go onto Etsy and buy Kajabi landing page templates. They are DONE and BEAUTIFUL. You just have to drop your goodness into them.

You're Welcome. :)

Don't let fear get in the way. This is going to support you and your work so beautifully!

ACTION STEPS:

- Imagine that landing pages are MAGIC and you are weaving that magic for others to play in!

- Can you create an email sequence that wraps people in YOUR love?

- Watch YouTube videos on HOW TO. I know you can do THIS!!!!

- Or… hire someone to do the tech, and you let God pour THROUGH you the messages for the landing pages and emails! :)

CHAPTER 28

CREATING YOUR FREEBIE

FREEBIES ARE FUN!!

FREEBIES ARE FUN!

Remember FUN makes creation so much easier.

Freebies are gifts.

And, if you are like me, giving gifts is one of my favorite things! Freebies are also one of the best ways to invite people into your business. There are plenty of free guides, eBooks, and handouts in the world. And, as great as those are, there is an opportunity to give something deeper and make more of an impact with your freebie.

If what you offer for free creates an experience for people, two things happen:

1. They get to have an experience or learn a tool that can literally shift their day and potentially how they live life.

2. They will now want more. They will want more of what you have to offer. If the one thing you gave for free made such a difference for them, then they will want to buy your book, your courses, your coaching, your products, etc.

So, as you sit in the creation of your freebie, I want you to be generous. What can you offer to people that will be filled with your energy, your wisdom, and your light? How can you serve at the highest degree and invite people to have a major shift in their life? This is what I want your freebie to be!

As always, the easiest way to create is by tapping into the Divine, so use your Sacred Creative Process and allow yourself to be a Vessel of Light. Enjoy this creation!

ACTION STEPS:

Ask God to show you what that experience can be.

And then CREATE it!

CHAPTER 29

NAME YOUR DATE

This is essential for everything you create. As you get closer to launching your podcast, your book, your digital course, your mastermind etc., there will be many things that want to distract you. These distractions will feel valid. They will feel real. But I am here to tell you that they are just illusions sent to you to keep you playing small.

FIGHT.

FIGHT for your brilliance.

FIGHT for your work.

FIGHT for your creations!

See these illusions like boats moving along the water. You can acknowledge them, you can notice them, but don't go aboard.

If your marriage starts to crumble the week before launch—don't believe it. It's an illusion that's here to stop you. If your kids are acting worse than normal, if your finances feel like they are diminishing, if your religious beliefs start to crack, or if anything else comes in like a freight train . . . I want you to keep walking.

Action defeats resistance.

CHAPTER 30

ACTION DEFEATS RESISTANCE

There is a "soft cast stage" that occurs right before we launch. I call it this because when I had 3 little boys under the age of 5, we had 3 broken bones in the span of 6 months! And, as annoying as casts were, the soft cast that the doctor puts on before the hard cast is the WORST. If you have had an experience with this, I know you are laughing.

The soft cast is put on the broken bone for 3 days while the swelling goes down. Once the swelling goes down, the hard cast is put on. But the soft cast stage is horrible because the arm is still broken. Totally fragile and not protected. Can you imagine how dangerous it is with little boys who have a soft cast on their arm? They still jump on couches and try to do front flips on the bed, all while having an ace bandage wrapped around their broken bone! It is the worse!

It is the same for us as we prepare to launch a creation into the world.

You may already have the episodes complete; you may have the image, the editor, and Libsyn connected, but you are not live yet… and you will want to delete it all!

You may have your book totally ready, edited and about to hit publish when you want to go back through the whole thing again and change 20 pages.

Your mastermind might be ready to launch, sales page created, images made, videos created, and you decide that you want to quit.

This is the soft cast stage.

Resistance comes in and will want to tear you apart. The distractions show up on a rampage.

I believe it shows up as a final attempt to stop you. And it can. But if you follow the simple practice of naming your date publicly, you will not shut down.

Why?

Because the momentum held in the listening of others will pull you propel forward. It will hold you accountable and resistance will not be able to stop you.

Steps to Naming Your Date:

1. Ask God what date your creation should go LIVE. Allow yourself to be in your sacred space, open your mind, and be willing to receive. You can place your hand on your forehead and close your eyes to receive the answer more easily.

2. Publicly share the date on Instagram and Facebook and with your email list. Share, share, share.

3. Get yourself out into the world with this date.

This will not only hold you accountable during the soft cast stage, but it will bring momentum into your world and help you finish what needs to be done with your creation.

What if everything isn't ready by that date? No problem! Use it as marketing content. Get on your social media platforms and email lists, and share! Tell them that you are fine-tuning it—that you are in deep creation—and give them a new date. Remember, everything always works at the perfect time in the perfect way under grace when you are directed by the Divine!

Now go forward and share that date.

Take a deep breath in.

The business strategy section is complete.

I have taught you the spiritual tools that I LOVE and use daily.

And now I am going to invite you to take my hand as I lead you into the miraculous world of healing....

This is my secret sauce.

HEALING ACTIVATES SUCCESS

Working with the Divine in your business is always going to be the magic ingredient to momentum and success.

And there is also a golden thread that will weave in the activation of success, every single day.

That golden thread is daily healing work. But how do you do daily healing work on YOURSELF if you don't know HOW to heal?

The truth is, we are all healers. It is an innate ability and gift that we have all been born with. But the language of healing was not taught to us. And so, it is a foreign language to most of us. Which means that we rely on outside sources to help us heal our own bodies.

I am not saying you shouldn't get outside support. I have an important team that helps me with healing work. I work with a Shaman AND a therapist, weekly. I know there are many blind spots that I cannot see on my own. But I also know that my body will speak to me, and that when I listen, I am able to clear out old beliefs and patterns to open the space for success; daily.

I want to support you with a few tools that you can begin to use daily to aid in your own personal daily healing work.

You might be wondering what this has to do with business and why it is here in this guidebook.

I will tell you that statistically, entrepreneurs don't have success on their side.

> *"According to data from the Bureau of Labor Statistics, as reported by Fundera, approximately 20 percent of small businesses fail within the first year. By the end of the second year, 30 percent of businesses will have failed. By the end of the fifth year, about half will have failed. And by the end of the decade, only 30 percent of businesses will remain — a 70 percent failure rate."*
> *- www. Entrepreneur.com*

There are many reasons why entrepreneurs fail. But my personal belief as to why they fail is because they get stuck in their old patterns, fears, and belief systems that keep them locked down and unable to flourish and succeed.

But, if you, as an entrepreneur are capable of doing your own daily healing work, *success will unfold.*

Imagine if you made a mistake in business (yes, I know that is hard to believe! LOL), and it ripped up a memory of a time when you failed at 7 years old. You are now creating and running business from that old programming that showed up when you were 7. The decisions you make won't be coming from the powerful and resourceful adult that you are NOW. They will be coming from that old, broken 7-year-old part.

Those old ways don't work for you now. They aren't going to support a million-dollar business. They are only going to keep you stuck. But, if you could activate healing in your body when the feeling of failure shows up, you will move forward with momentum and success and not get stuck and paralyzed with fear.

For most entrepreneurs, these old beliefs actually STOP their success. The success in business AND the success in IMPACT.

As a spiritual entrepreneur, we focus on both. Success in business and success in impact.

Instead of letting the past stop our growth, we heal through it.

Healing is the golden thread.

It is what allows us to expand into shapes we never knew were possible!

Doing a 5-10-minute healing practice every day can help clear out the limiting belief systems that have held you back.

Doing a daily healing practice can also awaken your gifts and allow your work to become more refined and powerful.

When we choose to do BIG things, create BIG creations and lead with light, we expand.

When we expand, our old belief systems, trauma and self-doubt will emerge.

Doing a daily healing practice will keep you in your highest vibrations and support you in your expansion with ease!

So, how do we begin this powerful practice? Let's start with understanding the basics of healing.

I want to support you in learning the language of healing, but I know you are busy!

You're an entrepreneur!

I could create 30+ pages on healing, but- you need the CliffsNotes version.

And so that is what I have created for you below.

Simple. Easy. Quick.

Healing for Entrepreneurs.

Here is what to expect and what you will learn:

1. What are Chakras

2. What happens when your chakra isn't functioning and what the results are when it is clear and clean

4. What essential oils connect to that distinct chakra

5. Healing Phrases to speak out loud to clear and activate that particular chakra

Healing is one of the foundational keys to success and making an impact in the world.

You will be learning the basics of healing within the chakras of your body and a few healing phrases that will clean out and activate healing with you.

WHAT ARE CHAKRAS:

Chakras are spiritual energy centers within your body.

When they get clogged up by daily life, old traumas, and negative energy- we don't get the results we want.

When we can clear and clean out the chakras, we exist in higher vibrations, and we get better results in life!

If you can imagine the wheel of a bike tire spinning as your feet push the peddles. If there was something lodged in the spokes of the wheel, the wheel would move slower or stop spinning completely.

Your Chakras are similar to this image. When they are energetically blocked, they don't function fully. When they are not functioning fully, they create negative results in our life.

When they are clean and cleared, the results are desirable and amazing!

Below are tables for you to reference to when you are doing your healing work.

It will be easy for you to know what Chakra to work on when you look at the tables. You can search by the negative results you are struggling with, and then do a healing phrase for that particular Chakra.

Or you can look at the positive results that you WANT to experience and speak a healing phrase for the Chakra that coordinates.

Through the daily Awaken healing practice we will be working with your main 7 chakras and 4 sub-chakras. They are all important and play a big role in bringing you back into wholeness.

CHAKRAS:

The Seven Main Chakras:

- The Root Chakra
- The Sacral Chakra

- The Front Solar Plexus

- The Heart Chakra

- The Throat Chakra

- The Third Eye Chakra

- The Crown Chakra

The Sub- Chakras:

- The Back Solar Plexus

- The Naval

- The Lungs

- The Back of the Head

LOOK AT THE IMAGE BELOW TO UNDERSTAND WHERE EACH OF THE 7 MAIN CHAKRAS ARE:

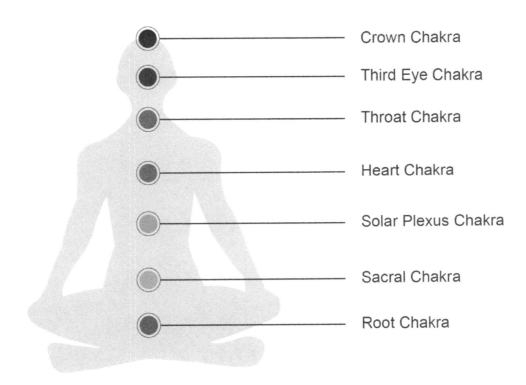

Crown Chakra

Third Eye Chakra

Throat Chakra

Heart Chakra

Solar Plexus Chakra

Sacral Chakra

Root Chakra

Are you ready to jump in?

TWO FEET... here we go!

UNDERSTANDING THE ROOT CHAKRA

ROOT CHAKRA:

Your Root Chakra is vital to your success, financially, physically, within your family, and emotionally. This Chakra literally roots you or keeps you scattered.

Essential Oils to use to support the Root Chakra:

- Douglas Fir

- Cardamom

- Myrrh

- Wild Orange

- White Fir

ROOT CHAKRA

UNBALANCED CHAKRA	BALANCED CHAKRA
➢ Scarcity and Lack	➢ Abundance
➢ Not Enough Money	➢ More Than Enough Money
➢ Negative Generational Patterns	➢ Creation of New Patterns
➢ Feeling Unsupported	➢ Feeling Immense Support
➢ Unhealthy Relationships	➢ Healthy and Strong Relationships
➢ Anger	➢ Contentment
➢ Trying to Survive	➢ Thriving
➢ Insecurity	➢ Security
➢ Feeling Like You Don't Belong	➢ A Deep Feeling of Belonging
➢ Fear	➢ Ease
➢ Feeling Unsafe	➢ Feeling Safety
➢ Addictions	➢ Freedom

HEALING PHRASES
FOR THE ROOT CHAKRA:

I breathe out and surrender that I
am unrooted and I do not belong.

I AM BREATHING IN AND
RECEIVING THAT I AM
ROOTED IN GOD AND I
BELONG.

Root Chakra

I AM ROOTED IN THE
DIVINE WITHIN ME AND
ABOVE ME. I AM HELD IN
LOVE, ABUNDANCE AND
SUPPORT.
I AM ROOTED.

I breathe out and surrender
that I am never enough.

I AM BREATHING IN
AND RECEIVING
THAT I AM ENOUGH,
AS I AM.

I breathe out and surrender that I don't have
any- (money, love, connection, joy, etc.)

I AM BREATHING IN AND
RECEIVING THAT I HAVE
AN ABUNDANCE OF
(MONEY, LOVE,
CONNECTION, JOY, ETC).

I breathe out and surrender that I am
unsupported.

I breathe out and surrender that I am
unsafe and afraid.

I AM BREATHING IN
AND RECEIVING THAT I
HAVE IMMENSE
SUPPORT.

I AM BREATHING IN
AND RECEIVING THAT I
AM SAFE AND AT
PEACE.

I breathe out and surrender any self-hate
and not accepting myself.

I breathe out and surrender that I am just
surviving.

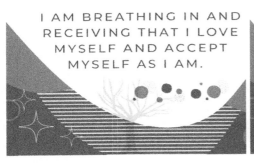

I AM BREATHING IN AND
RECEIVING THAT I LOVE
MYSELF AND ACCEPT
MYSELF AS I AM.

I AM BREATHING IN
AND RECEIVING
THAT I AM THRIVING!

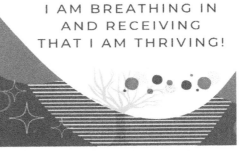

I breathe out and surrender any beliefs that say that I am stagnate.

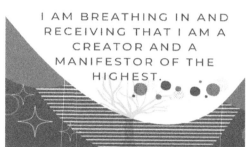

I AM BREATHING IN AND RECEIVING THAT I AM A CREATOR AND A MANIFESTOR OF THE HIGHEST.

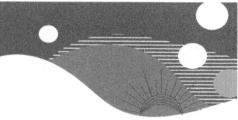

Root Chakra

I AM ENOUGH
AS I AM
AS I AM
AS I AM

UNDERSTANDING THE SACRAL CHAKRA

Today we are focusing on your Sacral Chakra. The color of this chakra is orange. It is located in lower abdomen. Your Sacral Chakra is the center of your creativity, your passion, courage, excitement, emotions, and sexuality.

This Chakra is such an important chakra around healing unhappiness, trauma, shame, and guilt. By healing the Sacral Chakra, you will find that you are free to feel happy, alive, creative, connected to life, and full of energy!

Essential Oils for the Sacral Chakra:

- Jasmine

- Litsea

- Copaiba

- Coriander

- Cypress

- Dill

- Blue Tansy

- Patchouli

SACRAL CHAKRA

UNBALANCED CHAKRA	BALANCED CHAKRA
➢ Depression	➢ Creativity
➢ Body Judgment	➢ Body Acceptance
➢ Apathy	➢ Passion
➢ Lethargy	➢ Excitement
➢ Fear	➢ Courage
➢ Unhealthy Sexuality	➢ Healthy Sexuality
➢ Rigidness	➢ Flexibility
➢ Unhappy	➢ Happy
➢ No Worth	➢ Worthy
➢ No Value	➢ Valued
➢ Shame	➢ Respect
➢ Trapped	➢ Freedom
➢ Indifference	➢ Ambition
➢ Doubt	➢ Belief
➢ Shut down	➢ Fully Self-Expressed
➢ Guilt	➢ Pride
➢ Stagnation	➢ Fulfillment
➢ Anxiety	➢ Peace

HEALING PHRASES
FOR THE SACRAL CHAKRA

SACRAL CHAKRA

I own my Divine Worth.
I feel my Divine Value.
I am Divine
As I am
As I am
As I am.

I breathe out and surrender
that sometimes I dislike my
body and do not accept it.

I BREATHE IN
AND RECEIVE
THAT I FULLY
ACCEPT AND
LOVE MY BODY.

I breathe out and surrender my
depression.

I BREATHE IN AND
RECEIVE MY
CREATIVE GENIUS.

I breathe out and surrender
everything that wants to quit and
is apathetic.

I BREATHE IN
AND RECEIVE
THAT I AM
PASSIONATE AND
TAKE ACTION!

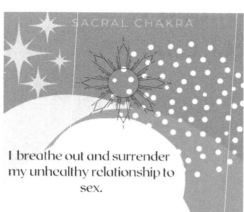

I breathe out and surrender my unhealthy relationship to sex.

I BREATHE IN AND RECEIVE A HEALTHY AND NOURISHED RELATIONSHIP TO SEX.

I breathe out and surrender all of my fear.

I BREATHE IN AND RECEIVE THAT I AM COURAGEOUS!

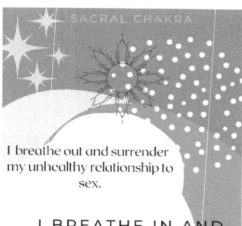

I breathe out and surrender my unhealthy relationship to sex.

I BREATHE IN AND RECEIVE A HEALTHY AND NOURISHED RELATIONSHIP TO SEX.

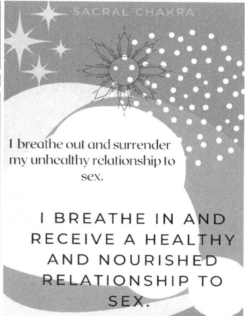

I breathe out and surrender my unhealthy relationship to sex.

I BREATHE IN AND RECEIVE A HEALTHY AND NOURISHED RELATIONSHIP TO SEX.

I breathe out and surrender everything that makes me question my worth.

I BREATHE IN AND RECEIVE I HAVE DIVINE WORTH.

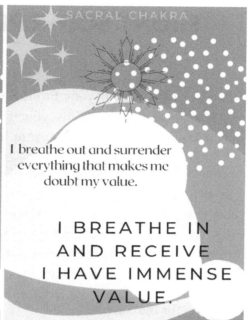

I breathe out and surrender everything that makes me doubt my value.

I BREATHE IN AND RECEIVE I HAVE IMMENSE VALUE.

I breathe out and surrender the belief that life is a struggle and full of hard work.

I BREATHE IN AND RECEIVE LIFE IS FULL OF PLAY AND EASE!

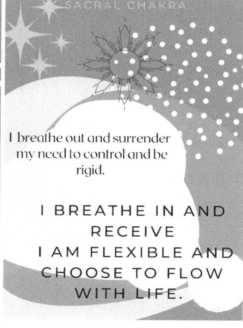

I breathe out and surrender my need to control and be rigid.

I BREATHE IN AND RECEIVE I AM FLEXIBLE AND CHOOSE TO FLOW WITH LIFE.

UNDERSTANDING THE
FRONT SOLAR PLEXUS CHAKRA

Today we are focusing on your Front Solar Plexus. The color of this chakra is Yellow. It is located right below your sternum bone. Another way to find this chakra is to count 3-4 fingers above your belly button.

Your Front Solar Plexus is the center of your energy, self-love, self-confidence, freedom, courage, and power. This chakra is a powerful chakra in your body. It is from here that you can really awaken your source of energy and power. It is in this space of your body that you can fully heal your self-confidence and self-love. When your Front Solar Plexus is cleaned out and balanced, you will find that you function better and can get the results you are looking in a profound way.

Essential Oils for the Sacral Chakra

- Juniper Berry

- Vetiver

- Ylang Ylang

- Lemon

- Basil

- Bergamot

 # FRONT SOLAR PLEXUS

UNBALANCED CHAKRA	BALANCED CHAKRA
➢ Low Self-Esteem	➢ High Self-Confidence
➢ Self-Doubt	➢ Self-Belief
➢ Self-Deprecation	➢ Self- Love
➢ Fearful	➢ Courageous
➢ Hiding	➢ Bold
➢ Powerless	➢ Powerful
➢ Being Controlled	➢ Freedom
➢ People Pleaser	➢ Speaking Your Truth
➢ No Will Power	➢ Will Power
➢ No Self-Control	➢ Self-Control
➢ Shame	➢ Pride
➢ Procrastinate	➢ Taking Action

HEALING PHRASES FOR
THE FRONT-SOLAR CHAKRA

Front Solar Plexus

I TAKE BOLD ACTIONS.

I BELIEVE IN MYSELF.

AS I AM
AS I AM
AS I AM

I breathe out and surrender everything that controls me.

I BREATHE IN AND RECEIVE I AM FREEDOM!

I breathe out and surrender all of my lack of will-power and self-control.

I BREATHE IN AND RECEIVE I HAVE AGENCY TO CHOOSE.

I breathe out and surrender my need to please others.

I BREATHE IN AND RECEIVE I SPEAK MY TRUTH.

I breathe out and surrender the
shame I place on myself.

I BREATHE IN
AND RECEIVE
I AM PROUD OF
MYSELF.

I breathe out and surrender
everything that wants to keep me
stuck and in procrastination.

I BREATHE IN
AND RECEIVE
I TAKE DIVINELY
INSPIRED
ACTION!

I breathe out and surrender all of
my exhaustion.

I BREATHE IN
AND RECEIVE
I HAVE PURE
SOURCE LIGHT
ENERGY.

I breathe out and surrender all of
my thoughts of self-doubt.

I BREATHE IN
AND RECEIVE
I BELIEVE IN
MYSELF.

I breathe out and surrender all of
the mean things I say to myself.

I BREATHE IN
AND RECEIVE
I LOVE
MYSELF.

I breathe out and surrender
everything that keeps me timid
and afraid.

I BREATHE IN AND
RECEIVE
I AM
COURAGEOUS!

I breathe out and surrender
everything that wants to keep me
hidden.

I BREATHE IN
AND RECEIVE
I AM BOLD!

I breathe out and surrender that I
feel powerless.

I BREATHE IN
AND RECEIVE
I AM
POWERFUL!

UNDERSTANDING THE HEART CHAKRA

Today we are focusing on your Heart Chakra. The color of this Chakra is green. The location of the Heart Chakra is within the physical space around your heart. This chakra is the beginning of us entering into the higher vibrational chakras. These chakras are more spiritual in nature and extremely powerful.

The Heart Chakra is the source of your unconditional love, your ability to receive, heal, have abundance, connection, trust, and total joy. You also experience gratitude, compassion, forgiveness, and empathy within this chakra.

As you heal the Heart Chakra, you will find these positive emotions flow through you and become a part of your life. If you have experienced trauma in your life, this will be where a lot of the pain is held. Don't be afraid of that pain. Moving through it will allow you to surrender it over and no longer need it.

This Chakra will help you receive more of everything. More love, more connection, more joy, more financial success, more clients, more peace, and more happiness. When you can truly let go of all the past experiences of rejection, then you can begin to receive. And when you can begin to receive, you will be able to receive all of the good you had been pushing away in the past. This is a powerful benefit to healing the Heart Chakra.

Essential Oils for the Heart Chakra:

- Geranium

- Eucalyptus

- Birch

- Bergamot

- Black Pepper

- Cassia

HEART CHAKRA

UNBALANCED CHAKRA	BALANCED CHAKRA
➤ Rejection	➤ Receiving
➤ Connection	➤ Isolation
➤ Acceptance	➤ Judgement
➤ Trust	➤ Distrust
➤ Self-Criticism	➤ Self-Love
➤ Unhappiness	➤ Total Joy
➤ Terror	➤ Safety
➤ Emotionally or Physically Sick	➤ Healing
➤ Not Enough	➤ Abundance
➤ Grudges	➤ Forgiveness
➤ Indifference	➤ Compassion

HEALING PHRASES
FOR THE HEART CHAKRA

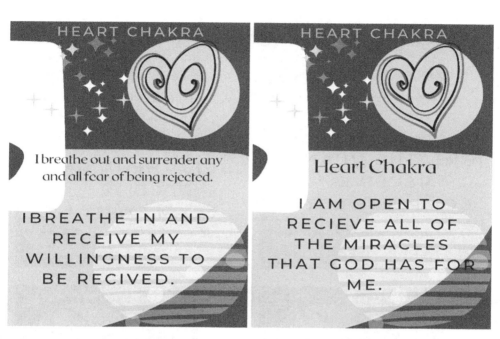

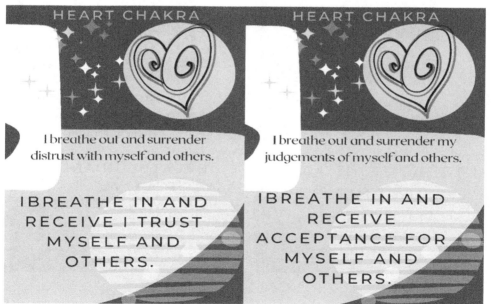

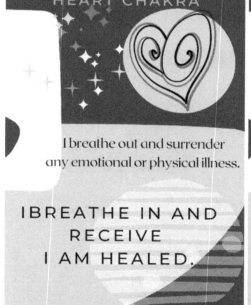

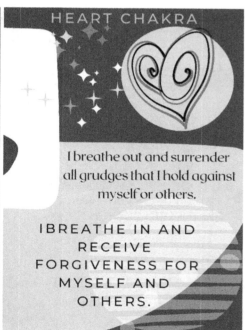

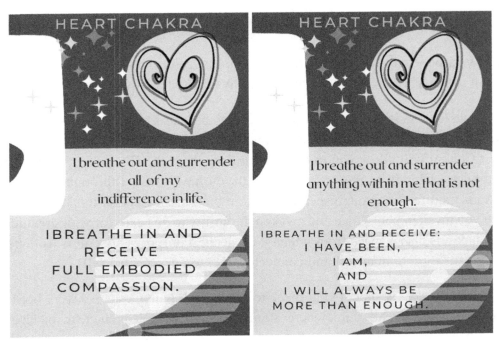

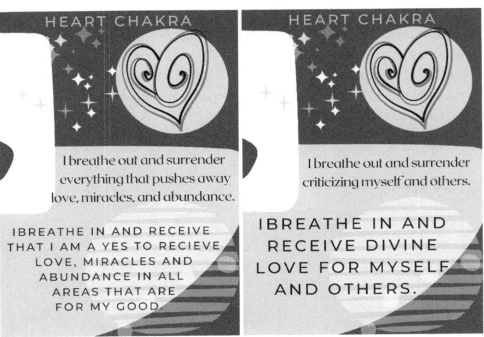

175

UNDERSTANDING THE THROAT CHAKRA

Today we are focusing on your Throat Chakra. The color of this chakra is blue. The location of the Throat Chakra is within the physical space of your throat.

The Throat Chakra is the source of your ability to be heard, seen, and acknowledged in this world. This Chakra opens up your deep power. Clearing and healing the Throat Chakra will allow you to speak your deepest truth. This chakra is also tied to the Sacral Chakra in the sense that what you have created through the Sacral Chakra is manifested through speaking it from the Throat Chakra. It is the space in which you awaken your voice and awaken the ability to be heard for your greatness. This Chakra is also a space from which your deepest purposes arise. It is from here that we can begin to manifest and connect deeper to our spiritual self.

The Throat Chakra is such a vital piece to our overall happiness. We were born to be seen and heard. But, somewhere along the line, we felt pain, fear, or shame around being seen and heard. And it was from there that we may have chosen to hide, stay quiet, and not "rock the boat." But we were meant to be disruptors! We were meant to speak our truths. This is how we feel our most self-expression and joy. This is how we connect with others and share our greatness. This is how the world will begin to change, one human at a time. When we all start speaking our truths and showing up in the world as the powerful beings we were created to be. This chakra is POWERFUL.

Essential Oils for the Throat Chakra:

- Lavender

- Cilantro

- Kumquat

- Spearmint

- White Fir

THROAT CHAKRA

UNBALANCED CHAKRA	BALANCED CHAKRA
➢ The Experience of Not Being Heard	➢ The Ability to Speak and Be Heard
➢ Wanting to Hide and Not Be Seen	➢ Stepping Forward and Allowing Yourself to Be Seen
➢ Staying Quiet	➢ Speaking your Truth
➢ People Pleaser	➢ Standing Up for Yourself
➢ Self-Rejection	➢ Self-Acceptance
➢ Living Without Purpose	➢ Living Rooted from a Purpose
➢ Feeling Trapped	➢ Liberated
➢ Blocked Communication	➢ Full Expression
➢ Holding Back Your Voice	➢ Articulate Communication
➢ Afraid to Speak	➢ Courageously Sharing
➢ Stuck	➢ Manifesting

HEALING PHRASES
FOR THE THROAT CHAKRA

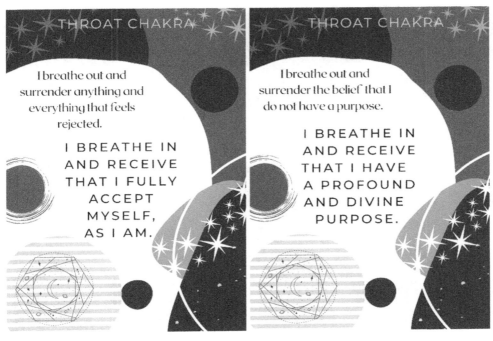

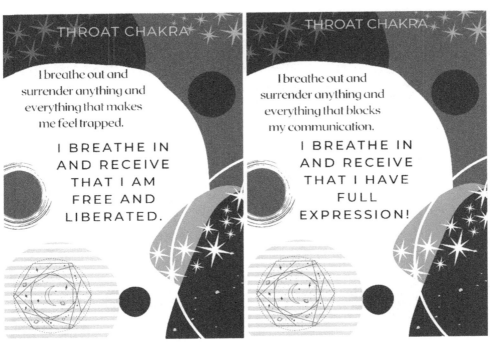

THROAT CHAKRA
I breathe out and surrender anything and everything that holds my voice back.
I BREATHE IN AND RECEIVE THAT I SPEAK POWERFULLY AND WITH EASE.

THROAT CHAKRA
I breathe out and surrender the fear of speaking boldy and courageously.
I BREATHE IN AND RECEIVE THAT I TRUST MYSELF TO SPEAK BOLDY AND COURAGEOUSLY.

THROAT CHAKRA
I breathe out and surrender everything that keeps me stuck.
I BREATHE IN AND RECEIVE THAT I AM A CREATOR OF THE HIGHEST ORDER. I FLOW WITH A GOLDEN RIVER OF MOMENTUM.

THROAT CHAKRA
I breathe out and surrender all the doubt and fear that tells me to hide my gifts.
I BREATHE IN AND RECEIVE THAT I BOLDLY SHARE MY GIFTS WITH THE WORLD, IN LIGHT AND CONFIDENCE.

UNDERSTANDING THE THIRD EYE CHAKRA

Today we are focusing on your Third Eye Chakra. The color of this chakra is indigo. The location of the Third Eye is on your forehead, between your eyebrows and right above your nose.

The Third Eye Chakra is the source of your spiritual gifts. It is here that you can access your spiritual gifts and awaken your true self. This is the gateway to your intuition, the Divinity within yourself, and spiritual vision. It is here that you are open to see spiritually and physically. Insight and wisdom are held within this space. Your spiritual brilliance is awakened when you heal this chakra.

The Third Eye Chakra is the sacred space that holds our gifts. It is in and through the Divine Light that we can access these gifts. It is through accessing them that our deepest JOY, LOVE, FREEDOM, and GUIDANCE is restored. It is where we are blessed with intuition, inspiration, support, grace, our true Divine self, connection to God, and the realm of LIGHT.

Essential Oils for the Third Eye Chakra:

- Frankincense
- Clary Sage
- Lemongrass
- Litsea
- Melissa
- Roman Chamomile
- Vetiver
- Wintergreen
- Ylang Ylang
- Rosemary

THIRD EYE CHAKRA

UNBALANCED CHAKRA	BALANCED CHAKRA
➢ Overanalyzing	➢ Intuitive
➢ Feeling Scattered	➢ Being Spiritually Centered and Rooted
➢ Fear of Your Spiritual Gifts	➢ Accepting Your Spiritual Gifts
➢ Resistance to Your Spirituality	➢ Standing Fully in Your Spirituality
➢ Refusal to See Truth	➢ The Ability to See Truth
➢ Feeling Dumb or Not Smart Enough	➢ Knowing and Feeling Your Deep Wisdom
➢ Playing Small in Life	➢ Access to Your Greater Self
➢ Confusion	➢ Mental Clarity
➢ Limited Perspective	➢ Enlightenment
➢ Controlling	➢ Surrender
➢ Willful	➢ Relying on the Divine Grace of God
➢ The Need to Be Right	➢ Teachable
➢ Excessive Self-Reliance	➢ Allowing Support
➢ Purposeless	➢ Purposeful
➢ Depression	➢ Inspiration
➢ Self-Confidence	➢ Trust Your Inner Voice
➢ Self-Doubt	

HEALING PHRASES
FOR THE THIRD EYE CHAKRA

Third Eye Chakra

I TRUST MY DIVINE
INTUITION.
I ACCEPT MY
SPIRITUAL GIFTS.
I AM WHOLE.

I breathe out and surrender
everything inside of me that is
confused.

I BREATH IN AND
RECEIVE I HAVE
MENTAL CLARITY

I breathe out and surrender
everything that needs to be in
control.

I BREATH IN AND
RECEIVE I AM A
YES TO
SURRENDER.

I breathe out and surrender
all of my willfulness.

I BREATH IN AND
RECEIVE I AM A
YES TO RELY ON
THE GRACE OF
GOD.

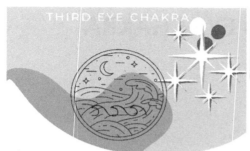

I breathe out and surrender all of my resistance to receiving inspiration.

I BREATH IN AND RECEIVE I AM A YES TO RECEIVE INTUITIVE INSPIRATION.

I breathe out and surrender all of my self-doubt.

I BREATH IN AND RECEIVE I TRUST MY INNER VOICE.

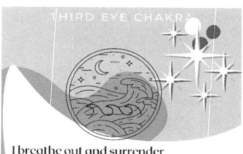

I breathe out and surrender my need to do it all alone.

I BREATH IN AND RECEIVE I AM WILLING TO ASK.

I breathe out and surrender anything and everything in me that overanalyzes and doubts my intuition.

I BREATH IN AND RECEIVE I HAVE PERSONAL ACCESS TO PURE, DIVINE INTUITION.

I breathe out and surrender being unrooted and scattered.

I BREATH IN AND RECEIVE I AM SPIRITUALLY CENTERED AND ROOOTED.

I breathe out and surrender all of the fear and resistance to my spiritual gifts.

I BREATH IN AND RECEIVE, I ACCEPT ALL OF MY SPIRITUAL GIFTS IN AND THROUGH THE DIVINE LIGHT.

UNDERSTANDING THE CROWN CHAKRA

Today we are focusing on your Crown Chakra. The color of this chakra is violet. It is located on the top of your head.

The Crown Chakra is where we connect to the Divine. It is where we are connected to our higher consciousness. This is where we have full spiritual clarity and awakening occurs. This is a very sacred space and it is always an honor to work in this space.

The Crown Chakra is our divine connection with God. This is where you open up and receive direction from the Divine. It is here where you can become still with yourself and feel more peace and clarity. This is a very sacred chakra. Not only will this awaken you spiritually, it will also awaken the healing of your stress levels and bring you more peace.

Essential Oils to Use for the Crown Chakra:

- Arborvitae

- Manuka

- Melissa

- Neroli

- Rose

- Spikenard

- Sandalwood

CROWN CHAKRA

UNBALANCED CHAKRA	BALANCED CHAKRA
➢ Disconnected from God	➢ Connected to God
➢ Empty	➢ Fulfilled
➢ Materialism	➢ Spiritual Devotion
➢ Despair	➢ Enlightened
➢ Cluttered Mind	➢ Clear Thinking
➢ Anxiety	➢ Peace
➢ Unhappiness	➢ Profound Happiness
➢ Doubting That you Can Receive From God	➢ Faith That You Can Receive from God
➢ Anger and Resistance to God	➢ Love and Acceptance of God
➢ Resistance to Living in Your Highest Vibration	➢ Accepting Your Highest Vibration
➢ Unsettled	➢ Relaxed
➢ Confused	➢ Guided
➢ Trauma	➢ Healing
➢ Overstimulated and Stressed	➢ Ease, Peace and Relaxed

HEALING PHRASES
FOR THE CROWN CHAKRA

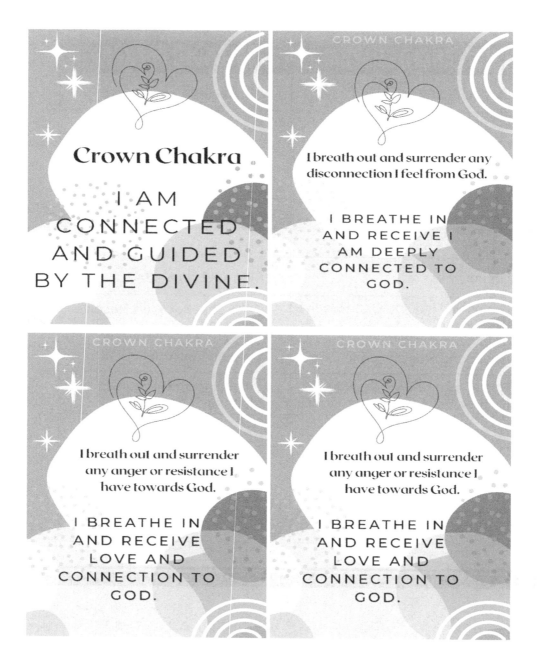

CROWN CHAKRA

I breath out and surrender the heavy thoughts of fear, doubt, noise and clutter in my mind..

I BREATHE IN
AND RECEIVE
CLARITY, PEACE,
AND FAITH.

CROWN CHAKRA

I breath out and surrender all of my overwhelm and stress.

I BREATHE IN
AND RECEIVE
EASE, PEACE
AND
RELAXATION.

CROWN CHAKRA

I breath out and surrender everything that feels empty inside of me.

I BREATHE IN
AND RECEIVE I
AM FULFILLED IN
MY LIFE.

CROWN CHAKRA

I breath out and surrender any and all confusion and fear.

I BREATHE IN AND
RECEIVE I AM
GUIDED BY THE
DIVINE, AT ALL
TIMES.

SUB CHAKRAS: UNDERSTANDING THE BACK SOLAR PLEXUS

We are now focusing on your Back Solar Plexus.

The color of this chakra is yellow, like the Front Solar Plexus. Most don't recognize this chakra as one of the main chakras, but I have found that it is one of the most important chakras to work with. It is located on the middle of your spine right below your shoulder blades.

Your Back Solar Plexus is the center of your warrior, strength, belief, faith, hope, freedom, courage and truth. This chakra has the power to heal you from all the different spaces of lies and illusions that run your limiting beliefs, and so much more. When your Back Solar Plexus is cleaned out and balanced, you will find that you have a deeper source of strength and power. Your ability to believe and have faith will be restored.

This Sub-Chakra is HUGE! Most of these negative qualities are things that most individuals deal with daily. I see over and over the power that comes from working in this chakra.

I believe that when you can clear this chakra out and restore it, you will have massive results!

BACK SOLAR PLEXUS CHAKRA

UNBALANCED CHAKRA	BALANCED CHAKRA
➢ Weakness	➢ Strength
➢ Victim	➢ Warrior
➢ Overwhelm	➢ Calm
➢ Stress	➢ Peace
➢ Feeling Trapped	➢ Freedom
➢ Doubt	➢ Belief
➢ Fear	➢ Faith
➢ Struggle	➢ Ease
➢ Hidden	➢ Shining in Your Light
➢ Shut Down	➢ Full Self-Expression
➢ Anxiety	➢ Peace
➢ Depression	➢ Joy
➢ Hopelessness	➢ Hope

HEALING PHRASES
FOR THE BACK SOLAR-PLEXUS

I breathe out and surrender everything that wants to shut me down.

I BREATHE IN
AND
RECEIVE MY FULL
SELF-EXPRESSION!

BACK SOLAR PLEXUS

I breathe out and surrender any and all stress.

I BREATHE IN
AND
RECEIVE I HAVE
PROFOUND PEACE.

BACK SOLAR PLEXUS

I breathe out and surrender any and all levels of depression.

I BREATHE IN
AND
RECEIVE I HAVE
ABSOLUTE JOY!

BACK SOLAR PLEXUS

I breathe out and surrender any and all hopelessness.

I BREATHE IN
AND
RECEIVE I HAVE
HOPE!

BACK SOLAR PLEXUS

I breathe out and surrender any and all fear.

I BREATHE IN
AND
RECEIVE I HAVE
COURAGEOUS FAITH

BACK SOLAR PLEXUS

UNDERSTANDING
THE LUNGS SUB-CHAKRA

The location is just as the name sounds. This sub chakra is held within the physical space of the lungs.

They hold the emotion of deep grief. True grief is held here, but the long-lasting grief that is centered on suffering is what we will be addressing.

The difference is that true grief is pure and moves through the body easier. Grief centered on suffering is long-lasting and brings us a lot of pain. Suffering is our experience of a situation, but not necessarily the truth of a situation. It is this experience of grief based off of suffering that creates so much pain in our lives. It is also what creates so many illnesses regarding the lungs.

LUNGS SUB-CHAKRA

UNBALANCED CHAKRA	BALANCED CHAKRA
➢ Grief	➢ Comfort
➢ Pain	➢ Soothed

HEALING PHRASES FOR THE LUNGS

UNDERSTANDING
THE NAVAL SUB-CHAKRA

The location of this sub chakra is right over the navel of your body. This is where we connected to our mothers in the womb and so, naturally, this is where we have healthy or unhealthy attachments, as well as our desire and will to live. Clearing out and restoring this chakra will bring you higher energy and restore your will to live FULLY.

NAVAL SUB- CHAKRA

UNBALANCED CHAKRA	BALANCED CHAKRA
➤ Unhealthy Attachments	➤ Healthy Attachments
➤ No Will to Live	➤ A Desire to LIVE!

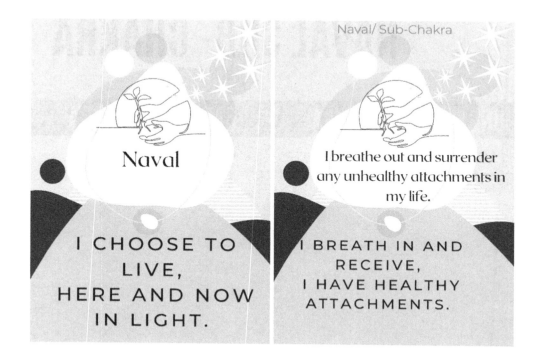

Naval/ Sub-Chakra

Naval

I CHOOSE TO
LIVE,
HERE AND NOW
IN LIGHT.

I breathe out and surrender
any unhealthy attachments in
my life.

I BREATH IN AND
RECEIVE,
I HAVE HEALTHY
ATTACHMENTS.

BACK OF THE HEAD

The back of the head is literally on the back of your head. It's right above where your neck and head join. If you were to cup your hand on the back of your head, this is exactly where it is located.

This is where we keep all of our negative thoughts. I like to call this the store house of the "chatter." When you clean and restore this space, you will not be bogged down with these negative thoughts. Instead, you will free from this noise and be present enough to create positive thoughts.

BACK OF THE HEAD SUB-CHAKRA

UNBALANCED CHAKRA	BALANCED CHAKRA
➤ Noisy Mind	➤ Clear Mind
➤ Negative Thoughts	➤ Positive Thoughts
➤ Fears and Doubts	➤ Clarity and Faith

HEALING PHRASES FOR THE BACK OF THE HEAD SUB CHAKRA

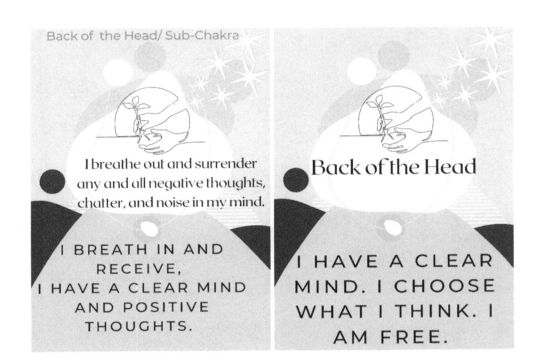

Back of the Head/ Sub-Chakra

I breathe out and surrender any and all negative thoughts, chatter, and noise in my mind.

I BREATH IN AND RECEIVE, I HAVE A CLEAR MIND AND POSITIVE THOUGHTS.

Back of the Head

I HAVE A CLEAR MIND. I CHOOSE WHAT I THINK. I AM FREE.

HEALING PHRASES TO WAKE UP MAGIC

You are a Priestess
of
Light.

YOU JUST
NEED TO
REMEMBER.

YOUR SOUL
KNOWS THE
TRUTH.

God is proud of you.
God sees YOU and
smiles with love.

YOU ARE A
BEING OF
LIGHT.

YOU ARE
NEEDED.

As you intentionally do a daily practice of listening to your chakras, clearing out the old beliefs and awakening new truths; success will open up.

You will see success in business and your personal life.

As you listen to the wisdom of your body; miracles will unfold.

You are the keeper of your gifts.

You are the weaver of magic.

As you heal YOU, everything else will fall into place with ease.

You are a healer, creator, leader, and entrepreneur.

Honor the voice of your body, and your body will honor you with energy and abundance!

MY DESIRE FOR YOU

My desire for you as we complete this book is simple. I want you to have success. When you are successful in business, you are also successful in the impact you make on this world.

Impact is how we change the world. You are here on this earth to make a shift that creates ripples of light. You are a leader who is ready to transform humanity. I know this because you wouldn't have been led to this book if you weren't.

And so, it is imperative that you have success. The world needs you to be successful. Your work is so deeply important. Your message, your gifts, and your insights will be the catalyst to many lives changing for the better.

I see you. I honor you. And I hold the space for you to rise as the brilliant leader, creator, author, and entrepreneur that you are.

You are ALL of these things and more. And I honor you for being both: AND. Both an entrepreneur AND a mother or father. Both a leader AND a human who needs to grocery shop and cook dinners. Both a creator AND someone who loves to dance in the car and sing at the top of your lungs. Both an author AND someone who is afraid and doubts.

You are ALL the things. That is what makes you so special and magical. Embrace ALL of you. Witness ALL that you do and focus on your magic. It is easy to see where we fall short in entrepreneurship. It is natural to look at the areas where we are failing, or the "to do" list that never gets complete. But, if you take the time to witness ALL that you ARE doing, and ALL of the magic that you hold—you will see miracles unfold.

WHAT WE FOCUS ON EXPANDS.

Focus on the success you already have had. If you made $50 today, focus on THAT! Focus on the miracle that you made $50! If you wrote a paragraph in your book, even when you wanted to write 2 chapters, focus on the miracle of the paragraph. Honor the words that DID come through. **See your small wins and make them BIG.**

When you see the miracles, more miracles will be magnetized into your life. Witness each one with gratitude and it will only expand and multiply.

Remember that you are not alone on this journey. You have a team of spiritual guides and angels who have agreed to walk with you. They are here waiting waiting for YOU to simply ASK for their support. When you lean in, soften your heart, and trust that they will show up—your business will become so much easier. The burden of holding it all by yourself will be lifted. The perfect clients will appear, and your work will become a place of miracles and light.

Create Sacred Space and go there each day. Commune with the Divine and LISTEN. You will begin to hear, see, feel, and know. Your muscle of receiving will strengthen and you will begin to be guided in every aspect of business and life.

Awaken the healer within you. As you take the time to heal, your life will flourish. The old belief systems and patterns that have kept you stuck in cyclical ways of being will clear out. The new ways—the fire, lava, changemakers ways inside of you—will rise and become your daily truths. Healing activates your gifts and clears out the path in front of you. You are a healer and the creator of your existence. As you choose to heal, you cultivate the soil of change in your world. As you witness your gifts rising, your ability to speak truth and watch it unfold into reality will be a daily experience. **Heal, and your business will succeed.**

Sprinkle seeds of magic wherever you walk. Pour out liquid gold whenever you speak. Breathe hope and belief into the world with each inhale and exhale.

You are more powerful than you can even comprehend. And with distinct intention and focus, you can literally change lives just by BEING.

BE YOU.

All of you.

The dark and the light. The fear and the faith. The doubt and the miracle worker.

Stop hiding.

When you hide, you hold your magic in dark corners where it only serves the dark.

When you throw your arms out wide, with your heart cracked open in faith, your gifts serve in the light. They reach the dark corners of other people's souls and remind that them that they, too, have magic.

Your willingness to share invites others to share. Your fearlessness awakens courage and hope in those who have been drowning in fear. When you stop hiding, you give others permission to do the same.

I love you.

I believe in you.

I see you.

I know your path has not been easy. I honor your desire to show up, again and again. Even with the daily struggles that you face—you have not given up.

And I believe you WILL succeed.

Partner with God in business and it will change every area of your life.

God became my business partner 5 years ago, and miracles have unfolded on every turn.

Lean in.

Full heart, full trust.

It may feel scary at first, but it will be the ride of a lifetime. You will see, hear, and witness God's hand in all that you do.

The lives you will change will exceed your wildest imagination, and the success that follows will be the afterthought.

My dear friend, we are partners on this journey. I honor your heart for the love that it holds. I honor your mind for the capacity it carries. I honor your faith and your courage. Even when it has felt like all was lost—you took another step and kept going.

You are a warrior.

Let us continue to RISE, to show up every day and lead in light.

God is My Business Plan.

Xo
Keira

GRATITUDE

I believe in support. I receive support from God and my Spiritual Team all day long. But I have invested around $200k in coaches, programs and more in the past 5 years.

Why?

Because I value receiving support.

I believe that there are people who know how to collapse time for me and my journey.

Below are all of the people who have taught me, coached me, loved me, supported me and their wisdom has found its way into my life and book.

Coaches in order of my entrepreneurial journey:

- Erin Matlock

- K.C. Baker

- Dr. Benjamin Hardy

- Shelagh Cummins

- Anna Kowalska

- Shaman- Eia

- Richie Norton

- Joe Polish

- And a massive amount of gratitude to my business partner/ current coach, Evan Carmichael

I am in the deepest gratitude for each one of these humans.

Thank you for seeing ME.

Thank you for believing in me.

Thank you for teaching me.

I have deep gratitude for my husband Dan who has been by side through this extraordinary transformation during the past 5 years.

He partners with me as I run multiple businesses and raise 5 kids.

Thank you, Dan, for supporting my WILD dreams and lava energy!

Books have also been my teachers and these authors have become energetic friends for me.

Below are a few of my favorite books

These books are like dessert to my soul and I know you will love them:

- "The Collected Works of Florence Scovel Shinn"

- "Think and Grow Rich," by Napoleon Hill

- "Change your Thoughts, Change Your Life" by Wayne Dyer

- "Momentum," by Evan Carmichael

- "The Magic" by Ronda Byrne

- "Illusions: The Adventures of a Reluctant Messiah" by Richard Bach

- "The One Minute Millionaire: The Enlightened Way to Wealth" by Mark Victor Hansen and Robert G. Allen

- "The Big Leap" by Gay Hendrickson

- "A Course In Miracles Made Easy" by Alan Cohen

- "The Compound Effect" by Darren Hardy

- "Breaking The Habit of Being Yourself" by Dr. Joe Dispense

- "The War of Art: Break Through the Blocks and Win Your Inner Creative Battles" by Steven Pressfield

- "Willpower Doesn't Work" by Benjamin Hardy

- "The Art of Learning" by Josh Watkin

- "Letting Go" by David R. Hawkins

- "Daring Greatly" by Brene Brown

- "The Biology of Belief" by Bruce H. Lipton

Made in the USA
Las Vegas, NV
11 September 2022

55081615R00125